The Technology Leaders

The Technology Leaders

How America's Most Profitable High-Tech Companies Innovate Their Way to Success

Peter S. Cohan

Jossey-Bass Publishers • San Francisco

Substantial discounts on bulk quantities of Jossey-Bass books are available to corporations, professional associations, and other organizations. For details and discount information, contact the special sales department at Jossey-Bass Inc., Publishers (415) 433–1740; Fax (800) 605–2665.

For sales outside the United States, please contact your local Simon & Schuster International Office.

Jossey-Bass Web address: http://www.josseybass.com

 Manufactured in the United States of America on Lyons Falls Turin Book. This paper is acid-free and 100 percent totally chlorine-free.

Library of Congress Cataloging-in-Publication Data

Cohan, Peter S., date.
    The technology leaders:how America's most profitable high-tech companies innovate their way to success/Peter S. Cohan.
        p.   cm.—(The Jossey-Bass business & management series)
    Includes bibliographical references and index.
    ISBN 0-7879-1072-4 (alk. paper)
    1. High technology industries—United States—Management.
    2. Technological innovations—Economic aspects—United States.
    I. Title. II. Series
    HD62.37.C64 1997
    620'.0068—dc21

          97-11674
          CIP

FIRST EDITION
HB Printing 10 9 8 7 6 5 4 3 2

The Jossey-Bass
Business & Management Series

To Robin, Sarah, and Adam

Contents

Preface

In the Darwinian struggle for profitable growth, we can learn from America's most highly evolved companies. Companies that come out on top of the fastest-growing, most rapidly changing, and most intellectually demanding markets have something to teach the rest of the business world.

America's most highly evolved companies are *technology leaders*. Technology permeates industry. It is the basis for many commercial and consumer products and is a key enabler for providing services. However, great technology alone is not enough to create a successful business. Uncounted billions have been spent developing technology that ultimately did not generate positive cash flows. On the other hand, a select group of technology entrepreneurs has become wealthy, converting tiny investments into vast personal fortunes. Part of this dynamic is a natural outgrowth of capitalism's cycle of creative destruction.

As they develop, many companies go through fairly predictable phases. Initially company founders rely on at most three sources of cash: personal money, paying customers, and possibly investment capital. To maintain positive cash flow they focus on external factors, such as changing customer needs, advances in technology, competitor strategies, and investor requirements. As these companies grow, they borrow money from banks, issue stock, create divisions, and acquire businesses and divest others. An unintended side-effect of their success is a distraction from the very behavior that created the success in the first place: the focus on maintaining positive cash flow by adapting to the needs of the marketplace.

In many cases, key decision makers delegate the responsibility for adapting the company to changing customer needs, advances in technology, and evolving competitor strategies. These executives spend increasing amounts of time mediating disputes over transfer pricing, arguing over executive compensation, trading businesses, redrawing organization charts, and catering to the needs of powerful board members.

The executives of the large company thus create an opportunity for a new generation of entrepreneurs to take away their customers. By the time they notice that anything has changed, they are years behind the "value propositions" offered by the new generation of entrepreneurs. Although these large companies are able to survive, often for many years, they have lost the strategic initiative in their industries and can only rely on cost reduction, not revenue growth, to enhance profitability.

Some large companies are able to transcend this cycle, however. Consider the recent histories of IBM and Hewlett-Packard (HP). Over the last decade, dramatic changes occurred in their markets, including the growing importance of the personal computer, the change from proprietary mainframe-based corporate computer systems to open client-server architectures, and the increased role of applications software.

IBM was unable to respond to these changes effectively. It remained dependent on the less robust proprietary mainframe business, ceded the personal computer operating system and application market to Microsoft, and focused management attention on internal reorganizations. Its senior executives were replaced, and its stock price, having peaked at 180 in 1987, dropped as low as 40 in 1993. Although IBM's financial position has recovered significantly under its new CEO, it remains to be seen whether the company will be able to retake the strategic initiative that it formerly enjoyed.

In contrast, HP combined its discovery of inkjet technology with an aggressive marketing strategy to build a 60 percent share of the $10 billion worldwide market for laser printers. HP also built a fast-growing line of UNIX-based computers to act as servers for networks of personal computers and workstations. Its share of the personal computer market is continuing to rise, with 90 percent of HP's revenues derived from products introduced within the last four years. Between 1991 and 1995, HP's stock price increased 480 percent.

What does HP do that IBM did not? This book explores how twenty technology companies, including HP, have sustained their success. The twenty companies were selected from a sample of 1,309 U.S. companies, based on their high R&D as a percentage of sales, their leading five-year average return on equity relative to their industry, and their reputation for innovative products and services.

These companies have a truly impressive track record. For example, they earned return on equity that was 2.4 times the U.S. industry median. They increased shareholder value at a rate 4.5 times that of the Barra Index of all U.S. securities. And they generated profits per employee that were 4.1 times the U.S. industry median. What is perhaps most impressive is that they were able to achieve all this profitability while increasing revenues at 5.7 times the U.S. industry median. Furthermore, during this five-year period, these outstanding companies generated earnings per share at a 43 percent compound annual growth rate, while the U.S. industry median actually dropped at an 11 percent rate.

The companies are Amgen, Cisco Systems, Compaq Computer, EMC Corporation, Gillette, Heartstream, HP, Intel, International Flavors and Fragrances, Johnson & Johnson, Merck, Micron Technology, Microsoft, Minnesota Mining, Oracle, Parametric Technology, Schlumberger, Synopsys, Thermo Electron, and U.S. Robotics.

The most important factor that keeps these twenty companies ahead of the pack is the way they adapt to change. Rather than deny that change is taking place, these technology leaders look for ways to exploit change for the benefit of their customers. If this change means that some products must become obsolete, the firms cannibalize ruthlessly. And technology leaders don't just cannibalize their products, they even uproot their most fundamental business processes.

Technology leaders work with a mental model that guides their strategic decisions. In this model (see Figure P.1), people and technology are combined to create products that customers are eager to buy. These products generate capital and insight: the capital comes from the products' operating profit, and the insight is the result of feedback from customers and competitors and the firm's success in its core business processes (such as, new product development and product supply). Through resource allocation, technology leaders channel this capital and insight into new product development projects and business process redesign.

By optimizing this model, technology leaders create a success cycle that leads to ever greater levels of capital and insight. Technology leaders expand this success cycle through four sources of

Figure P.1. Technology Leaders: Flow of Capital and Insight.

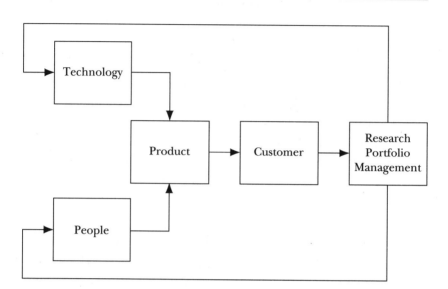

advantage, which are the critical management practices that drive their superior performance.

1. *Entrepreneurial leadership.* Technology leaders identify, attract, and motivate the smartest people to perform to the limits of their ability. How do they do this? They have CEOs who combine a deep understanding of technology with an intense drive to make money. They use values-based visions that grab smart people and pull them in the right direction. This contrasts with peer companies who try to motivate people by exhorting them to "maximize shareholder value." Technology leaders have open organizations and take a humanistic approach to managing people. However, technology leaders have some hard edges. They are highly competitive, and they pay people to perform. They often balance below-average cash compensation with stock options that are valuable only if the company's stock price keeps going up.

2. *Open technologies.* Technology leaders get the technology that meets the needs of their customers. In this pursuit, they often pay for quick access. If they have the technology inside the company, they will invest to make it even more valuable to customers. If the technology is available from outside the firm, they will get access

to it. This access could range from acquiring a company to licensing the technology from the people who developed it. Technology leaders seek a strong market position in specific "leverage-point technologies" that will allow them to organize third parties in pursuit of an industry standard. And technology leaders assign people to monitor new technologies before they become a dangerous threat. At the same time, they catalog their noncore technologies and outplace them, while selectively "renting" technologies that are needed only for specific projects.

3. *Boundaryless product development.* Technology leaders combine their people and technology in a process that generates superior value for customers. They form cross-functional teams. They work with early adopters to understand their unmet needs. They develop prototypes based on these needs. And they modify these prototypes based on customer feedback. Furthermore, they create "product supply" capabilities that enable them to meet mass-market demand while maintaining high product quality and delivery-time standards.

4. *Disciplined resource allocation.* Technology leaders use the capital and insight that results from their successful products to expand their success cycles. They use resource allocation to spread organizational learning. They screen projects using portfolio grids. They build project time lines for the most attractive projects, being sure to incorporate specific exit ramps. They estimate success probabilities and incremental net cash flows between decision nodes. And they systematically reallocate resources to the projects with the greatest expected value.

Target Audience

This book is intended to help practitioners understand these four sources of advantage. CEOs, chief technology officers, division managers, product managers, scientists, and engineers in technology-intensive industries can use this understanding to help them manage the linkages between technology and markets. Venture capitalists, investment and commercial bankers, and other investors and financial intermediaries can use the findings of this book to help identify potentially valuable technology investments. CEOs, division managers, and product managers in industries that are less technology-intensive can also use the strategies presented here to help them increase their return on innovation.

Overview of the Contents

Chapter One explores the key opportunities and threats that face technology-intensive industries, highlighting how these trends affect technology organizations, from the CEO to the engineers. It details the analytical approach used to select the twenty technology leaders. The chapter also explores the four sources of advantage that drive the companies' outstanding performance and shows how these sources of advantage contribute to their ever-expanding economic value.

Chapter Two examines the first key source of advantage *entrepreneurial leadership.* It provides insights into the leadership styles of David Packard (HP), Roy Vagelos (Merck), and Bill Gates (Microsoft). The chapter explores the evolution of effective decentralization through examples from HP, Cisco Systems, and 3Com. It describes how Cisco Systems and others attract and retain top people. And it illustrates the powerful financial incentives that enable Thermo Electron and Microsoft to create valuable new businesses. Chapter Two concludes by describing a process that CEOs can follow to embed these principles in their own organizations.

Chapter Three scrutinizes the second source of advantage that distinguishes technology leaders: *open technology.* Technology leaders follow a five-step process that enables them to nourish and renew the technology essential to their ability to compete. The chapter shows how technology leaders Cisco Systems and Compaq forge industry standards and illustrates how Synopsys, Johnson & Johnson, Merck, and HP monitor new technologies. It describes how Microsoft and Cisco Systems partner or acquire (or both) to close the capability gap. Chapter Three concludes by outlining a change process that CEOs can use to adopt the practices that are so effective for technology leaders.

Chapter Four explores how technology leaders "rent" technologies that they need for a specific project, presenting examples from Amgen and Intel. It uses an example from Louis Dreyfus to illustrate the principle that managing technology is a form of arbitrage. The chapter shows how technology leaders structure "rental agreements" that give them access to technologies that enable them to pursue a business opportunity with transient value—without requiring a permanent investment. It highlights the many pitfalls to such arrangements and presents a road map that describes how best to manage them. Chapter Four concludes by showing how this road map has contributed to the outstanding performance of Cisco Systems.

Chapter Five shows how technology leaders blend their people and technology through the third source of advantage: *boundaryless product development*. It describes a five-step process that enables technology leaders to get new products to market that customers want to buy. The chapter shows how this process has helped HP, Microsoft, Schlumberger, Gillette, and U.S. Robotics achieve great results. It explores how mechanical and semiconductor product companies have achieved quantum improvements in product cycle times through the use of prototyping software developed by Parametric Technology and Synopsys. And it shows how CEOs can incorporate what works for technology leaders into their own companies.

Chapter Six zooms in on the most critical element of boundaryless product development: how technology leaders *create value for customers*. This chapter introduces the concept of the "value triangle." It argues that the way companies connect the corners of the value triangle determines their product's success. The chapter illustrates this principle with examples from EMC Corporation, International Flavors and Fragrances, and Heartstream. Chapter Six concludes by describing a process that technology leaders follow to create value for customers, illustrated with examples from 3Com and Cisco Systems.

Chapter Seven examines the fourth source of advantage: *disciplined resource allocation*. Technology leaders view resource allocation as a process of betting under uncertainty. All the capital and insight generated by the other three sources of advantage are invested through the resource allocation process. To win the game, technology leaders follow five principles that help them manage the risks in their research portfolios. Chapter Seven illustrates these principles using an example from the pharmaceutical industry, based on one company's actual experience. And it shows how technology leaders make each of these principles work.

Chapter Eight integrates the first seven chapters by presenting an *Innovation Scorecard* comprising clusters of questions that can help readers see how their own organizations compare to those of technology leaders. Readers will be able to gauge their company's relative performance in terms of return on innovation, leadership, technology, product development, and resource allocation. The chapter also suggests some of the ways companies can collect the data needed to answer these questions. It concludes by describing an approach that CEOs can use to make their organizations more innovative.

Chapter Nine offers some thoughts on the future. It discusses how technology leaders may change the general business landscape and describes the implications of these changes for managers, workers, consumers, and financiers.

My Relevant Experience

My interest in this topic springs from more than fifteen years of experience consulting to technology developers and users. I have worked with clients in software, telecommunications, semiconductors, on-line information services, biotechnology, chemicals, oil refining and marketing, and oil services. I have helped these clients address such issues as market and product development, R&D portfolio management, joint venture design and implementation, and technology licensing. I have worked with clients that sell technology and have managed teams that use technology to make business processes respond more effectively to customers.

In my experience, the major cause of failed technology ventures is the inability or unwillingness of technologists to appreciate how their products will create value for customers. The importance of this issue parallels the switch in the computer industry from proprietary to open operating systems. When technological skill was scarce, companies that controlled it could dictate the direction of their markets—customers would have no choice but to buy what the engineers designed. As computing power was decentralized, technological skill was more widely dispersed. Because of their large embedded bases, many technology companies needed to experience a serious crisis to become aware of the fundamental shift in their markets from technology-push to customer-pull. Many of my consulting projects have been intended to help clients cope with this shift.

In 1995, I worked on a research report that studied a set of R&D leaders, the objective being to learn how these R&D leaders addressed certain key issues. The study explored how to strike the appropriate balance between the business and technology sides of an enterprise, how to introduce profitable products ahead of competitors, how to value technology resources, how to maximize the productivity of the R&D organization, and how to optimize the value of the R&D portfolio.

The success of this project motivated me to further explore these fundamental business issues. I wanted to test the validity of these findings on a larger set of companies across a broader spectrum of industries. And I hoped to distill from this research a set of principles that could be vividly illustrated to help managers in all industries.

Acknowledgments

This book could not have been written without the help of many people. I am grateful to all the executives and venture capitalists who offered me their views on the topics discussed here, including Dean Morton (HP); Bob Saldich and John Midgeley (Raychem); William Draper (Draper International); Kevin Compton (Kleiner, Perkins); Geoff Yang (International Venture Partners); John Morgridge (Cisco Systems); Victor Grijalva, Brian Clark, and Bernard Gremillet (all of Schlumberger); Michael Griffith (In-Stat); Alan Levy (Heartstream); John Bush (Gillette); George Heilmeier (Bellcore); Eric Benhamou (3Com); Aart de Geus, Kurt Keutzer, and Paul Lippe (all of Synopsys); Maureen Lawrence (Whitetree); and Andy Clark (Eastman Chemical).

I also appreciate the help of my colleagues Bruce Henderson (Matrix USA), Bob Stringer (Sherbrooke Associates), Jeff Coburn (Coburn Consulting), Geoff Fenwick (Renaissance Solutions), Tom Lynch (Lazard Frères), Eric Stang (Raychem), Ryan Englund (Monsanto), Dennis Harp (Alex. Brown), Peter Laino (K-III Communications), Jake Wesner (McKinsey & Company), Mordechai Fester (Cisco Systems), Richard Yanowitch (VeriSign), and Chuck Roush. And I am very grateful for the support and encouragement throughout this project of Cedric Crocker, Cheryl Greenway, and Byron Schneider of Jossey-Bass.

Finally, I would like to offer special thanks to my wife, Robin, who patiently reviewed each chapter of this book and offered many insightful comments from her experience in the trenches.

May 1997   PETER S. COHAN
                                              East Marlborough, Massachusetts

The Author

PETER S. COHAN is president of Peter S. Cohan & Associates, a management consulting firm. His strategy consulting practice helps companies in technology-intensive industries identify, evaluate, and exploit new business opportunities. The firm's services include proprietary research reports, management development, and process facilitation. Clients are global leaders in such industries as telecommunications, on-line information services, computer networking, biotechnology, pharmaceuticals, and oil services.

Cohan's investment consulting practice works in partnership with leading private-equity investment firms to capitalize on specific "industry buildup" strategies. For example, in a sector of the financial services industry, his firm is executing a strategy to acquire companies, consolidate operations, and distribute products through a low-cost channel. He has also made seed capital investments in the Internet software business.

Cohan worked at CSC/Index with James A. Champy, coauthor of *Reengineering the Corporation,* and at the Monitor Company, a strategy consulting firm cofounded by Michael E. Porter of the Harvard Business School. Cohan also worked as an internal consultant in the banking and insurance industries.

Cohan received an M.B.A. degree (1985) from the Wharton School; did graduate work in computer science at the Massachusetts Institute of Technology, where he studied with Dr. Michael Hammer; and earned a B.S. degree (1980) in electrical engineering from Swarthmore College.

Cohan can be contacted at Peter-Cohan@msn.com.

The Technology Leaders

Chapter One

The Technology Leaders and Their Sources of Advantage

Think about your company and answer these questions:

Does a high percentage of your current revenues and profits come from new products?

Do leading customers consider your products to be the industry standard?

Do your products rank first in market share?

Do you know what your core technologies are and what they're worth?

Does your company monitor new technologies and capitalize on the opportunities they create, even if it cannibalizes existing products?

Does your company excel at forming and managing profitable partnerships?

Have you successfully acquired and integrated other companies to fill gaps in technology that your customers require?

Are your scientists and engineers the best in the industry?

Is your company ranked first in your industry in profits and sales per employee?

Do you follow a disciplined process for shifting resources to the product development projects with the highest expected value?

Have your investments in innovation contributed substantially to your company's value?

If you answer these questions affirmatively, then you probably work for a *technology leader.* If not, this book will show how your company can improve its performance by forging tight linkages between your technology and your markets in response to changing customer needs, competitor strategies, and technologies.

Technology leaders participate in technology-intensive industries. They generate a stream of profitable new products that account for a substantial portion of current year revenues. And they lead their industries in five-year average return on equity.

Although technology leaders recognize that generating profits is an essential element in sustaining their survival, maximizing shareholder value is not their primary focus. Although they are aware of their competitors, they do not allocate their resources to eliminate them. Although they are careful to assess the applicability of their core competencies to the requirements of a new market, technology leaders do not build their strategies around their core competencies. Finally, technology leaders avoid the massive firings that are often couched as resulting from reengineering. In fact, they focus on attracting and retaining the best people, not on eliminating wasteful business processes.

Technology leaders concentrate on understanding the needs of their customers. This focus leads to products that meet customer needs better than the competition. Because many technology products are so complex, technology leaders try to make the customer's purchase decision as simple as possible. Technology leaders excel at assembling pieces into a standard system that offers a "turnkey" solution at the lowest life cycle cost. By forging and controlling the industry standard, technology leaders gain the largest share of the market.

To sustain their positions, technology leaders compete effectively for the best scientists and engineers. Just as there are great differences in market share between the standard bearers and the rest, so are there tremendous productivity gaps between the best scientists and engineers and the pack. Technology leaders devote substantial management effort to identifying, hiring, and retaining the very best people. As we will see in Chapter Two, even a company's physical location can be an important part of its strategy for winning the best people. For example, by locating its headquarters in Redmond, Washington, away from the densely high-tech-populated Silicon Valley area, Microsoft raises the costs of competitors who might want to hire away its best employees.

Because technology leaders have built large organizations that do create value for customers, while adapting to rapidly changing customer needs, technologies, and competitor strategies, they are the most highly evolved companies in the ecology of business. The single most important attribute that keeps technology leaders on top is their intellectual humility. Because they are so keenly aware of how quickly their markets can change, technology leaders constantly search for information that helps them reinvent themselves to create more value for customers. As a result, I believe that all organizations can benefit from a greater understanding of these technology leaders.

The Dynamics of Technology-Intensive Industries

Companies that participate in technology-intensive industries are exposed to a powerful set of industry forces that make it difficult for them to maintain high levels of profitability:

Rapidly changing technology often undermines incumbents. IBM's position in the computer industry, buttressed by the central role of its proprietary mainframes, was substantially undermined when Microsoft took control of the operating system for the personal computer. Now, Microsoft's position in PC software could be threatened by the network computer (NC). This concept, advocated by Oracle, Sun Microsystems, and others, consists of a $500 "thin client" device that rapidly downloads information and targeted office applications from the Internet. The success of the NC may depend on whether its lower maintenance costs outweigh the costs of rewriting PC-based corporate applications. As a technology leader, Microsoft is quietly hedging its bets by developing products and services that can profit from the NC concept, should it evolve into a significant market.

Barriers to entry in many technology-intensive industries are low. These changes in technology come from unexpected places because barriers to entry are so low. If a smart person has a great idea, it doesn't take much capital to make it into a successful product. For example, the kernel of Linux, a clone of the UNIX computer operating system written for Intel-based personal computers, was coded largely by a single person—Linus Torvalds, living in Helsinki, Finland. The supporting code that made Linux a complete operating system package was contributed by hundreds of volunteers scattered around the globe, connected via the Internet (Klaus, 1993).

The traditional role of patents as a means of building a moat around intellectual property has substantially eroded. Patents certainly play a role in the pharmaceutical industry, where investments in developing new products can reach as high as $400 million, thereby making a seventeen-year patent protection essential to recouping this investment. In virtually all other technology-based industries, however, by the time a patent has been approved, the state of the market may be several generations beyond the technology being patented. In other words, companies in technology-intensive industries are no longer able to rely on patents to protect their leadership position. They are much better off investing in a work environment that successfully attracts and retains top people who introduce profitable new products to the marketplace ahead of the competition. As we will see in Chapter Four, on the other hand, patents have value for high-tech companies—as a bargaining chip in swapping technology with competitors.

In many technology-based industries, companies that create and control an industry standard enjoy market positions that result in very high profitability. A classic example of this is Microsoft's establishment of MS-DOS and Windows as the industry-standard operating system. Working with Intel and other developers, Microsoft leveraged its position in operating systems to build a profitable position in a range of software products. Given the low barriers to entry into the software industry in particular, a large number of small companies can develop software to solve specific problems. Corporate customers need to minimize the risk of purchasing software from a vendor who may not be able to adapt to their changing needs. They also need to minimize the cost of rewriting their application programs and retraining their employees. In these markets, the emergence of a standard that is perceived as minimizing these risks and costs confers tremendous market power on its creator(s).

The pressures on existing firms to keep pace with these changes has resulted in record levels of mergers and acquisitions. Technology executives are increasingly realizing that the risk of being left out of an industry-transforming technology is substantially greater than the cost of acquiring a company that has established leadership in that technology. Several years ago, AT&T's $11.5 billion acquisition of McCaw Cellular was driven by the realization that building a national cellular network would be much more time consuming and costly than buying the company. Similarly, the $4 billion purchase of StrataCom by Cisco Systems resulted from a similar calculation for acquiring ATM (asynchronous transfer mode, a relatively fast, though expensive, data communications standard). For Cisco Systems, this purchase represents one in a long string of acquisitions designed to give its customer base a complete suite of networking products that work together.

In many technology-based industries, the "horizontal negotiating leverage" has shifted from technology suppliers to technology consumers. An essential element of the success of Hewlett-Packard (HP) and Digital, for example, was that engineers designed product for the engineer sitting at the next bench ("the next bench paradigm"). Because these companies created an environment that attracted and retained the best engineers, other engineers who bought these products were happy to have their product needs dictated to them. However, as a result of the shift to open operating systems, the creation of more efficient channels of distribution, and the growing importance of selling computers to consumer markets, the next bench paradigm was fundamentally altered. More specifically, these trends created an opportunity for buyers to compare the products of a wider array of vendors. Customers used their purchasing leverage to force a dramatic reduction in the overall cost of purchase and use while demanding steady improvements in performance. Whereas HP responded effectively to this change, particularly in laser printers, Digital's performance lagged HP, partially as a result of its inability to respond to changing customer needs. This shift has also influenced the pharmaceutical industry, as exemplified by Merck's $6 billion purchase of Medco, a high-volume buyer of pharmaceutical products for managed care programs.

Companies in technology-intensive industries continuously reevaluate their core technologies. This process has led to dramatic growth in strategic alliances among companies seeking to limit the risks associated with participating in new markets. For example, HP negotiated a strategic alliance with Intel to develop a 64-bit CPU that HP was unwilling to finance itself. These alliances, however, are inherently unstable, creating significant management challenges as companies find themselves simultaneously cooperating and competing with each other in different markets. For example, Microsoft agreed to allow America Online to establish itself on its Windows 95 operating system in exchange for America Online's agreement to use Microsoft Explorer, a World Wide Web browser. In this deal, Microsoft was simultaneously trying to increase the market penetration for its Web browser while helping the company that is in competition with its Microsoft Network on-line information service.

Implications for CEOs, Chief Technology Officers, and Others

These trends have unique implications for CEOs, chief technology officers, division managers, product managers, and engineers.

CEO

As CEO of your company, you will need to ask yourself the following questions: How do the changes in my industry affect the attractiveness of the markets in which we compete? How do these changes influence our competitive position in these markets? Should we be selling or outsourcing some of our businesses or functions? Are there important technologies that we should acquire or license, rather than build internally? What impact do these changes have on the value of our assets, including our research portfolio? In light of these changes, are our managers and other employees the right individuals to achieve our business objectives? Are we working on the right product development projects? Do our financial and other incentives create an environment that reinforces the importance of achieving these objectives?

Chief Technology Officer

As chief technology officer, you need to answer the following questions: Do we have the right balance between "technology" and "business" in our research organization? How good are we at introducing profitable new products to the market ahead of our competitors?

What are our core technologies, and are we maximizing their value? What are our noncore technologies, and are we managing them to balance efficiency and access? Are we attracting and retaining the best scientists and engineers, and are we maximizing their productivity? Do we understand the value of our research portfolio, and are we taking a systematic approach to reallocating people and capital from the less valuable to the most valuable projects?

Division Manager

Division managers have been forced to deal with a set of issues that are similar to those facing CEOs, only on a smaller scale. How much should division managers look for ways to share capabilities with other divisions in order to enhance the company's overall performance? Will division managers and employees be appropriately rewarded for their participation in cross-divisional projects?

Product Manager

To what extent will the organization recognize the enhanced importance of managing cross-functional teams? In particular, will the organization create the kinds of financial and other incentives necessary to facilitate the coordination of engineering, manufacturing, marketing, sales, and finance to introduce profitable new products ahead of competitors?

Engineer

How will these competitive challenges affect the status of engineering? Whereas engineering traditionally enjoyed a position at the top of the functional hierarchy, will it now be required to share high status with other functions, possibly manufacturing and marketing staff? Will engineers continue to have the opportunity to advance their professional interests and push the state of the art, or will the work be focused exclusively on applying less advanced technology for more immediately marketable products? Will the company reward engineering as its role becomes more commercial, or will engineers seek employment with other organizations, where staying on the cutting edge of technology is more highly valued?

Twenty Technology Leaders

To gain perspective on these issues, I studied how twenty leading technology companies have addressed them. The research included interviews with CEOs, chief technology officers, project managers, engineers, industry analysts, and academics. It also included a review of publicly available information, including financial reports, product literature, published interviews with executives, and articles written in trade magazines and general business publications.

These outstanding companies were selected based on three criteria. First, they compete in *technology-intensive industries,* as measured by R&D expense as a percentage of sales. In the sample of companies examined for this book, this percentage varied from 2.2 percent (Gillette) to 22.1 percent (Synopsys). The twenty companies in the sample had an average R&D-to-sales ratio of 8.3 percent, 2.6 times the average for all U.S. industry ("Annual Report on American Industry," 1996).

Second, these firms *outperform their peers* in terms of profitability, productivity, and shareholder value creation. In the twenty companies studied for this book, five-year average return on equity ranged from 12.4 percent (Thermo Electron) to 56.2 percent (Cisco Systems). These companies also lead their industries in terms of profit per employee. The top twenty companies ranged from $11,400 per employee (Thermo Electron) to $194,100 per employee (Cisco Systems). They created substantial increases in shareholder value, as measured by percentage change in stock price over five years. This increase ranged from as low as 9.3 percent (Schlumberger) to as high as 4,667 percent (Parametric Technology).

Finally, these twenty companies have earned a *reputation for innovative products and services* that customers want to buy. In fact, several of the companies that were selected have performed less well in purely financial terms. However, these technology leaders have sustained their reputation for renewing themselves through the creation of innovative new products. Schlumberger, 3M, and HP are three companies that were included principally due to their reputation for successful product innovation.

The twenty technology leaders include five in various types of computer hardware (Cisco Systems, Compaq, EMC Corporation,

HP, and U.S. Robotics); four in different types of computer software (Microsoft, Oracle, Parametric Technology, and Synopsys); two in semiconductors (Intel and Micron Technology); two in pharmaceuticals (Merck and Johnson & Johnson); one in medical electronics (Heartstream); two in consumer products (Gillette and International Flavors and Fragrances); one in biotechnology (Amgen); one in oil services (Schlumberger); one in energy, environmental services, and medical products (Thermo Electron); and one diversified in consumer and commercial products (3M).

Four Sources of Advantage That Drive Leaders' Success

The focus of this book is to understand how these twenty technology leaders sustain their outstanding performance. In particular, we explore the four sources of advantage that drive their high rates of return on innovation (Figure 1.1).

Return on innovation refers to the net present value of investments in innovation: the discounted cash flows resulting from expenditures on researchers, laboratory facilities, prototypes, and other research investments, netted against the cash inflows generated by the new products that result from these research investments. Return on innovation has not been widely used as a measure of research productivity; however, it has conceptual advantages over at least one popular measure: the percentage of current-year revenues from new products. Unlike the latter measure, return on innovation reflects the level and timing of the costs required to develop, manufacture, and distribute new products as well as the timing of the cash inflows that result from their sale.

These four sources of advantage are management practices that enable the most successful technology companies to outperform their peers.

Entrepreneurial Leadership

Technology leaders, though many are quite large, have figured out how not to lose the entrepreneurial spirit. Technology leaders ruthlessly uproot the weeds of bureaucracy and internal politics before they can choke the vigor out of the organization. How do they accomplish this?

**Figure 1.1. Four Sources of Advantage
That Drive Return on Innovation.**

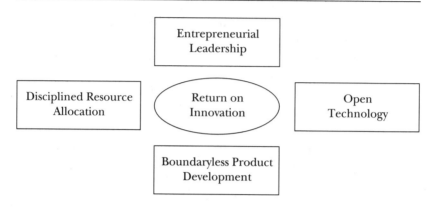

Their CEOs understand technology and business. The most profitable technology companies are run by CEOs who understand both technology and business. Bill Gates is the best example of this. As one Microsoft employee noted, Gates is the only person he has met who combines a deep understanding of technology with a 100 percent bottom-line orientation.

Peer companies are often run by CEOs who are strong on technology and weak on the business side. Occasionally, a CEO who is seen as strong on the business side (particularly consumer marketing) but weak on technology is brought in to save a technology company.

They identify and recruit the best people. Technology leaders compete effectively to hire the best people. They use their experience to identify the characteristics of people who will continue to push the edge of the technological envelope. They want people who not only have technical smarts but who can work effectively in a team of functional specialists to achieve corporate business objectives.

Peer companies on the other hand, often hire scientists and engineers with excellent technical skills but not necessarily the organizational skills required to work effectively in a cross-functional team.

They provide entrepreneurial financial incentives. Technology leaders create opportunities for their people to generate substantial personal wealth. In some cases, these incentives are stock options in the company. In other cases, workers get substantial equity in a "spinout" from the parent company. Peer companies reward engineers and scientists by allowing them to keep their jobs.

They create a winning culture that rewards innovation. Technology leaders design their psychological incentive systems to reward innovation. Their financial systems measure the incremental contribution to corporate revenues and profits from new products. Their performance evaluation and promotion processes reward innovation. They communicate the importance of innovation by repeating stories of successful innovators within the company and hold corporate events that celebrate innovative scientists. They allow their scientists to devote part of their time to pursuing personal business interests.

Peer companies may talk about the importance of innovation but may, for example, promote individuals who are more effective at internal politics than at creating new products that customers value. Peer companies often create "dual career ladders" that, when announced, are intended to provide managers with an opportunity to advance for managerial accomplishments while technical people are promoted for technical accomplishments. In fact, these dual career ladders offer higher compensation to individuals who progress up the managerial path.

They create mechanisms that undermine complacency. Technology leaders recognize that perhaps the greatest enemy they face is an internal one: the complacency that results from resting on their laurels. In order to fight this enemy from within, they often create teams that compete with each other to design, develop, and commercialize new products targeted at the same market. This internal competition is often more fierce than the threat from external competitors. By making competing teams aware of each other's progress, these companies spur teams on to even higher levels of performance. Peer companies view internal competition as wasteful and rarely engage in the practice.

Open Technology

Technology leaders reject the "not invented here" syndrome. Rather than try to develop all technologies in-house, they take an open approach. Technology leaders focus first on meeting the needs of their customer base. If they can meet customer needs out of their research portfolio, they will do so. If not, they will forge alliances or make acquisitions to ensure that their customers get the technology they need. How do technology leaders manage their technologies?

They identify their core technologies. Technology leaders invest significant management time to identify their core technologies, namely those that help the company create products with attributes that customers value, that are competitively unique and difficult to replicate, and that are applicable to a wide range of markets.

Peer companies often assume that their current technologies are core technologies. Because they are so comfortable with this assumption, they don't bother to analyze the technology in terms of its ability to create unique customer value or its applicability to a wide range of markets.

They look at themselves from the outside in. Technology leaders also view their current technologies from the perspective of current and potential customers. Technology leaders identify technologies that they currently lack but that should be part of their core because customers want them.

Peer companies often perceive that if they do not have a technology in their portfolio, it must not be worth having. As a result, peer companies are often blindsided by substitute technologies.

They identify their alliance technologies. Technology leaders identify their noncore or alliance technologies—those technologies that the firm possesses that are no longer needed, or those that the firm does not possess but needs to "rent" for a specific project. Because peer companies often suffer from the "not invented here" syndrome, they believe that any technology invented outside the company is worthless.

They maximize the value of their core technologies. Technology leaders invest in their core technologies to keep them competitively unique. They also seek out new markets they can enter by leveraging their core technologies. Furthermore, technology leaders acquire companies that enjoy market leadership in technologies that they believe should be in their core.

Peer companies often allow their core technologies to languish, assuming that prior success will lead inevitably to future success. Furthermore, peer companies find it difficult to monitor advances in technology that could undermine their current business model.

They syndicate their alliance technologies. Technology leaders create organizations that are dynamically permeable. In other words, they open up noncore elements of their technology portfolio to the outside. This opening up may take the form of shedding noncore technologies through layoffs. Often this shedding can result in the creation of a new venture, partially financed by the company, that enables the firm to maintain its access to the technology. These new ventures also create goodwill by providing former employees with an entrepreneurial opportunity.

Conversely, technology leaders may choose to rent certain noncore technologies as needed for specific projects. This may be accomplished in a variety of ways, from hiring a technical consulting firm to structuring and managing a strategic alliance with a competitor.

Peer companies, on the other hand, may believe that they should build a moat around their company. They may engage in the effort to identify their core technologies but then subsequently decide not to shed their noncore technologies. This decision leaves them with fewer resources to invest in their core.

They monitor and update their core technologies. Technology leaders recognize that changes in technology, competitor strategies, and customer needs can threaten individual products as well as their whole approach to doing business, so they establish mechanisms for monitoring these changes. They build networks of relationships with industry participants to gather market intelligence systematically.

Technology leaders use this information to reassess their core technologies *and* to take appropriate action. On the other hand, peer companies may look for new technologies only from their existing competitors. More important, peer companies may not use the information they collect to change their business. They may recognize and respond to fundamental change only after its cost has been substantial.

Boundaryless Product Development

Boundaryless is an awkward-sounding term with a very important meaning. Technology leaders try to eliminate boundaries. They minimize the unproductive rivalries between internal functions and reduce barriers between themselves, customers, suppliers, and even, in some cases, competitors. How do they accomplish this?

They build cross-functional teams. Technology leaders build a team that involves all important constituents for the new product. Depending on the specific requirements of the project, these teams might include representatives from key suppliers, "early adopter" customers, engineering, marketing, sales, manufacturing, finance, and purchasing. Team members understand the project vision, participate in the development of project goals, and formulate a specific plan for achieving these goals. Furthermore, team members believe, based on senior management's support, that their success will be rewarded. In some cases, as we will see with the HP inkjet example in Chapter Five, they believe that failure could cost them their jobs.

Peer companies pursue a more linear, "relay race" approach: engineers develop blueprints that are "thrown over the transom" to manufacturing, then to sales, then to the customer. The failure to integrate across functions creates additional costs due to hand-offs and rework. It frequently delays market introduction and often limits customer acceptance.

They seek "early adopter" input. Technology leaders work with early adopter customers to gain an in-depth understanding of their product requirements. This understanding is developed early in the process, as an input to the product design. Customer input is not limited to verbal descriptions of vaguely articulated needs; it is concrete and relates to the way customers actually use current products. Technology leaders specifically link these customer requirements to the attributes of the new product.

Peer companies, on the other hand, may develop their products based on the interests of the dominant function, typically engineering. Often, peer companies wait until the product has been manufactured to perform customer research that will be used to estimate sales volumes.

They use iterative prototypes. Technology leaders build prototypes very early in the development process. These prototypes help the team identify and resolve many internal issues before too much money and time has been spent. For example, prototypes help technology leaders assess how costly it may be to manufacture the product. Prototypes may also help gauge the quality, cost, and availability of key product components at an early stage in the development process.

Technology leaders also use prototypes to get feedback from early adopters, which is then used to modify the product design. The prototype also unites the team and gives senior management a clear sense of project status.

Peer companies, on the other hand, often hand off an engineering model to manufacturing once the design is "complete." And in many peer companies, the engineering model is not optimized for manufacturing. As a result, manufacturing often asks engineering to redesign the product to lower its manufacturing cost.

They build product supply capacity to satisfy mass-market demand. Technology leaders create manufacturing and distribution networks that satisfy mass-market volume, delivery-time, and quality requirements. Peer companies, on the other hand, often develop an innovative product that languishes within a small sector of the market, creating an opportunity for a technology leader to capitalize on the product's full economic potential. Another problem that faces peer companies is that they do not have sufficient manufacturing and distribution capability to meet the growing demand for their product. This creates significant ill-will among customers, making it difficult to maintain industry leadership.

Disciplined Resource Allocation

Although some technology leaders have a less scientifically rigorous approach to resource allocation than others, they all enforce a corporate discipline that results in an efficient allocation of scarce capital and human resources. What's different about how technology leaders allocate resources?

They use the resource allocation process to promote organizational learning. Technology leaders build project postmortems into their resource allocation process. This internal feedback leads to changes in business processes that shorten product development time and increase customer value. Technology leaders also update their research project decision trees to reflect the most recent state of a project's expected value. Peer companies, on the other hand, often look at project setbacks as an opportunity to reorganize.

They use portfolio grids to screen projects. Technology leaders use portfolio grids to link their research projects to their corporate strategy. These grids compare projects along dimensions that are important to senior management. For example, technology leaders analyze the profit potential of particular market segments and the company's competitive position after the product has been introduced to the market.

Projects that are targeted at market segments with low profit potential or with a weak competitive position are screened out. Projects targeted at market segments with high profit potential and strong competitive position continue to receive corporate resources.

Peer companies often continue to fund research projects that intrigue scientists and engineers, and their executive sponsors, regardless of potential market impact.

They build project time lines for high-potential projects. Technology leaders develop a standard approach to project management that they apply to each project in their R&D portfolio. Project teams develop time lines that indicate how long they think each project phase will take to complete. At the end of each phase, project teams estimate how likely it is that the project will continue to the next phase. Teams also estimate the incremental net cash flows of continuing to the next project phase.

Peer companies may have a more casual approach to building project plans that make it difficult for senior management to compare projects.

They reallocate resources to projects with the greatest expected value. Technology leaders calculate the expected present value of their research projects. If a project does not meet predefined performance standards at a specific project phase, it is canceled. Technology leaders then free up the capital and people to work on more valuable projects. Technology leaders recognize that not all projects will succeed, and the people involved in the terminated project are usually not penalized for their participation.

Peer companies, on the other hand, lack a disciplined review process; projects are often canceled or funded based more on who in the company is sponsoring the project.

Linkage with Return on Innovation

As discussed earlier, return on innovation is the present value of the cash flow components of a research project, including (1) cost of feasibility research; (2) cost of licensing-in technologies for the project, if any; (3) cost of prototype development, including usability and manufacturability testing; (4) cost of regulatory testing, if applicable; (5) cost of incremental production facilities, if any; (6) cost of incremental product distribution network, if any; and (7) the contribution margin of the new product resulting from the research project over its life.

In order to calculate return on innovation for an entire company, the return on innovation for all its projects is added together, including the costs associated with research projects that do not result in marketable products.

The four sources of advantage all work together to increase the value of the firm. They reduce wasted spending and shorten product cycle times, thus accelerating the cash inflows from new products. They even increase the magnitude of the cash flows from new products.

Entrepreneurial leadership ensures a steady stream of new products—and the positive cash flows that they generate—while managing the growth in the cash outflows associated with the research staff.

• *Decreases cash outflows.* Technology leaders have fewer people, being paid lower base salaries and doing more work. As a result, they have lower employee cash costs than their peers.

• *Shortens time to generate cash inflows.* Technology leaders can get products to market in less time. Highly motivated, smart people are able to focus their energies intensely on achieving ambitious project deadlines without sacrificing product quality.

Open technology broadens the markets into which technologies are sold, bringing more cash into the company. Technology leaders shed or outplace noncore technologies, thereby turning off the cash spigot to lower-return technologies. And they outsource alliance technologies, which helps increase the cash inflows from new products by getting better products to market faster. It also limits the firm's costs for technologies that the company needs for only a short time.

• *Decreases cash outflows.* Technology leaders stop spending on technologies that have outlived their ability to create value for customers, channeling the cash thus saved to technologies with greater potential to create value.

• *Shortens time to generate cash inflows.* Technology leaders reduce product cycle times. Rather than delay a project to develop a key technology internally, they license it from a third party. As a result, technology leaders get products to market faster and begin generating positive cash flow sooner.

• *Increases magnitude of cash inflows.* Technology leaders get incremental sources of cash by finding new markets for core technologies and by licensing out noncore technologies in exchange for royalties or other fees.

Boundaryless product development increases return on innovation by decreasing cash outflows, shortening time to market, and increasing operating profit.

• *Decreases cash outflows.* Technology leaders don't incur the extensive rework associated with the relay race approach to product development. Thus they eliminate the costs associated with redesign to ease manufacturing and to increase market acceptance.

- *Shortens time to generate cash inflows.* Technology leaders shorten the time from the start of the project to product launch. Again, they shorten time to market by eliminating rework associated with missed handoffs in the relay race approach. This speeds up the time to generate positive cash flow and, because the cash is received earlier, increases its value to the company.
- *Increases magnitude of cash inflows.* Technology leaders produce and market products that are more successful in the marketplace, thus generating more operating profit.

Disciplined resource allocation increases the magnitude of the positive net cash flows that the research portfolio will generate. It also shifts resources out of projects with unacceptable prospects for success, thus minimizing cash outflows.

- *Decreases cash outflows.* Technology leaders cancel projects with limited potential before too much money has been spent. Investment in innovation is thus targeted at projects with the highest potential returns.
- *Shortens time to generate cash inflows.* By ensuring that the most promising projects are not deprived of resources, technology leaders complete projects more quickly. Products get to market faster and begin generating operating profits sooner.
- *Increases magnitude of cash inflows.* By supplying the most promising projects the capital and other resources they need, technology leaders create more successful products, increasing their operating profit.

Chapters Two through Seven explore these four sources of advantage in greater detail. These chapters describe the key principles that guide technology leaders and provide examples of how technology leaders apply these principles. They also suggest steps that companies can take to incorporate these principles into their own organizations.

Chapter Two

Entrepreneurial Leadership

Leading Silicon Valley venture capitalists and executives in many top technology companies emphatically agree that effective leadership is the most important contributor to superior performance. Simply stated, if a company hires the best people and puts them to work on the right things, the company will succeed. How can a company identify who the "best" people are? How can it attract and retain these people? How can it create a working environment where these people produce at their highest level? Technology leaders use the following management approaches to address these issues:

- *Effective leadership.* Although it is probably impossible to train an individual to adopt the behaviors of a leader, effective leaders drive their companies to respond pragmatically to the demands of the market.
- *Winning culture.* Technology leaders create cultures that attract and retain top people.
- *Top team players.* Technology leaders identify and hire the best people in their fields.
- *Decentralized decision making.* Technology leaders recognize that, as companies grow, founders cannot make all the decisions themselves.
- *Entrepreneurial incentives.* Technology leaders link employee work performance, the value of the company, and employee net worth in a powerful combination that motivates employees to build successful new businesses.

Effective Leadership

The source of the extraordinary success of top technology companies is their unusually effective leaders. Leaders are people who get the right things done. In top technology companies, leaders have a deep understanding of technology. But the best leaders also have the business vision to see how that technology can create value for customers and returns to shareholders.

High-tech companies differ from low-tech companies primarily in the way they approach the "soft side" of leadership. More specifically, successful high-tech companies follow five principles of leadership: three "soft" principles that differ from low-tech companies and two "hard" principles that are the same. The "soft" principles are the following:

1. *Values-driven visions.* Successful high-tech companies create visions that reach deep into the "collective values" of the people in the organization. Values-driven visions relate these values to the social good that the organization strives to create, contrasting sharply with the more mundane exhortations to "maximize shareholder value" that low-tech companies use. Values-driven visions grab employees by the heart and drive them to work hard to achieve the objectives of the organization.

2. *People-oriented rhetoric and action.* Successful high-tech companies tailor their rhetoric and action to create an environment that attracts and retains what they perceive to be the best employees. This principle is important because aspiring high-tech leaders compete aggressively for scarce, highly educated, young engineers and scientists who want to work on products that make a difference in the marketplace.

3. *Open organizations.* The most successful high-tech companies are open and flexible. Because the pace of change in their markets requires rapid response, successful high-tech CEOs lead with their knees bent. They get involved with customers. They use informal teams. They are talkers and listeners. Unlike many low-tech companies that produce reams of formal customer satisfaction surveys and then do nothing with the results, high-tech leaders use customer input throughout their product development processes to change their designs before the product hits the market.

The two "hard" principles that high-tech leaders share with their low-tech peers are as follows:

1. *Achievement orientation.* High-tech industries are intensely competitive. In order to win, high-tech leaders must supplement the respect for individuals, described previously, with an intense focus on beating a specific competitor. High-tech leaders often create internal competition that is focused on creating the best product for the customer.

2. *Entrepreneurial incentives.* The most successful high-tech CEOs recognize that top people are motivated not only by respect for the individual and making a difference to society. High-tech leaders understand that top people are competitive and that they measure their achievement by how much money they have earned. Through the use of stock options and performance-linked bonuses, these CEOs provide their people with the chance to share in the success that they help create.

The following descriptions of David Packard, Bill Gates, and Roy Vagelos illustrate these leadership principles.

David Packard

David Packard cofounded Hewlett-Packard (HP) in 1939 and helped build it to become an employer of 105,000 people in 120 countries by 1996. Many people who worked with him claimed that his values, "the HP Way," contributed substantially to the company's success (Mitchell, 1996). These values included trust and respect for people, focus on contribution and quality, a promise to conduct business with uncompromising integrity, a commitment to teamwork, and a belief that people need to be flexible and innovative.

In addition, Packard developed such management practices as "management by walking around," decentralized decision making, open offices with few doors, and the refusal to take on debt to finance new ventures. During World War II, when HP's annual sales averaged about $1 million and the company could have gained additional business, David Packard decided not to bid on several large government contracts. The reason, he said, was that to fulfill the contracts, HP would need to hire people who would have been fired when the contracts were completed. Packard asked his employees to call him Dave. He never remodeled his 1950s office at HP headquarters; it had a brown linoleum floor and a relatively plain desk and chairs (Mitchell, 1996).

According to Bill Krause, CEO of Storm Primax and founder and former chairman of 3Com, Dave Packard was a great leader, in part because he was both a "hard-headed" man when it came to business matters and a "soft-hearted" man when it came to people matters. In 1970, after having just been promoted to be HP's first district sales manager for computers, Krause had a serious car accident requiring him to be in the hospital for sixty to ninety days. While laying in his bed that evening worrying about whether or not he would be able to keep his job, much less his new promotion, the telephone rang. Dave Packard had called to reassure Krause that his boss would fill in for him while he was recovering and that he would be able to keep his district sales manager position.

On the other hand, while giving a presentation as the HP 3000 worldwide marketing manager in 1978, Krause was reviewing some customer satisfaction issues. The same Dave Packard interrupted Krause and made it crystal clear to him that if he could not deliver the highest level of customer satisfaction, he would be replaced. This comment grabbed Krause's attention and made it very clear what the performance standard was ("Quotes on David Packard," 1996).

Bill Gates

Bill Gates cofounded Microsoft in 1975 and by 1996 had increased its market capitalization to the point where his 23 percent share of the company was worth over $20 billion, making him the world's wealthiest individual. As *Microsoft Secrets* (Cusumano and Selby, 1995) points out, much of the company's performance stems from Gates's technical and business acumen, as well as his leadership and managerial abilities. His talents are reflected in both his ability to understand software and computers and his ability to create and maintain a highly profitable business.

Microsoft employees and observers from outside paint similar pictures of Gates. They describe him as a visionary with a maniacal drive to succeed, accumulate great power, and make money by taking advantage of his technical knowledge and understanding of industry dynamics.

According to Jim Conner, program manager of the office product unit, Gates is unique in that he combines an exceptionally brilliant intellect with a complete focus on creating wealth (Cusumano and Selby, 1995).

According to Dave Maritz, former test manager of Windows and MS-DOS, Gates is a maniac. He knows more about the product than any of his employees. Microsoft people go into meetings and come out sweating, because if there is any flaw, Gates will land on it immediately and pick it to bits (Cusumano and Selby, 1995).

According to a *New Yorker* article by John Seabrook (1994), IBM seriously underestimated Gates. The company dismissed him as a technically adept, but naive, kid. By the time IBM finished negotiating with Gates, however, they realized that he had decimated them with his thirst for power and profits and his innate knowledge of contract language.

Roy Vagelos

Former Merck CEO Roy Vagelos brought powerful ideas to Merck that helped focus its research on the development of some very valuable products. Vagelos was also an inspirational leader.

Looking *one hundred years* into the future, Vagelos described the enduring role of purpose at Merck. He asked his audience to imagine what Merck would look like in the year 2091. While the company's strategy and methods would be different, Vagelos believed that its people would continue to be inspired by the same timeless dream of helping people and relieving suffering (Collins and Porras, 1994).

Jeffrey L. Sturchio, Merck's director of science and technology policy, reinforced the power of this vision by contrasting his prior employer with Merck. Sturchio noted that the biggest difference between the two was the alignment between words and actions. At Sturchio's other employer, management gave speeches about values and visions but failed to back these words with actions. At Merck, however, rhetoric and action were the same (Collins and Porras, 1994).

Despite the differences in their personal styles, Packard, Gates, and Vagelos share important attributes: they combine an understanding of technology with the business skills required to make a profit from it; they recognize the market power of developing the industry-standard product and marshal their resources persistently to attain this power; they command the respect of very talented individuals and persuade them to work to the limits of their skills; and they have the intellectual humility to recognize that new technologies can undermine their basic business models—changes that simultaneously threaten the survival of the business and provide new profit opportunities.

Although it is unlikely that the extraordinary skills of these leaders can be transferred to others, there are more basic leadership initiatives that CEOs of technology companies can take that will help improve performance. Dr. George Heilmeier, CEO of Bellcore, suggests that technology CEOs should consider the following ideas (Heilmeier, personal communication, July 21, 1996):

Put your chief technology officer (CTO) on the board of directors. Although many companies place their chief financial officer (CFO) on the board, fewer provide board seats to their CTOs. Companies that do put CTOs on their boards strengthen their ability to evaluate technology investments and the business risks and opportunities associated with new technology.

Spend significant CEO work time on technology. Although many CEOs talk about the importance of technology to their business, they may tend to spend most of their work time doing the things that they are most comfortable with, depending on the function from which they emerged.

View R&D as an investment, not an expense. Many CEOs, particularly during the first half of the 1990s, viewed R&D as an expense to be cut rather than as an investment in the future growth and profitability of the company. Technology leaders, as will be described in greater detail in Chapter Seven, view R&D as an investment.

Define the CTO role clearly. Chief technology officers should be skilled at unstructured problem solving. They should provide broken-field thinking for fundamental business problems such as how to lower product and process costs and how to increase revenues. CTOs should be held responsible for achieving one or two bold initiatives each year that have the potential to transform the company. In addition, "discovery research" projects should be required to generate at least one useful deliverable each year. These prototypes should be useful for marketing and business people within the company. Finally, CTOs should be part of the worldwide scientific community so that they can better read the weak, but relevant, signals from technology areas that could affect their company.

Show an interest in R&D. The CEO should hold periodic breakfasts and lunches with the CTO to discuss progress on important projects. CTOs should identify topics that can be presented to the board. CEOs should create a sense of enthusiasm within R&D by taking an active interest in its activities.

Winning Culture

Top technology companies create cultures that attract the best people and motivate them to produce products that win in the marketplace. As with leaders, identifying the attributes of a winning culture does not make it easy for competitors to replicate that culture. With that as a caveat, the cultures of top technology companies share the following attributes: they expect people to work in teams, to express their opinions, and to respond constructively to fact-based criticism; they foster a healthy degree of internal competition—believing that it is better to "eat your own young" than to feed it to the competition; they reward innovation in pursuit of superior "customer value propositions"; and they create an informal work environment that stimulates creative people. 3M, Microsoft, and Oracle all provide interesting examples of winning cultures in technology companies.

3M

At 3M, a company that epitomizes innovation, one of the early CEOs, William McKnight, developed a set of innovation principles that were further enhanced by subsequent generations of management (Loeb, 1995). These guidelines have enabled 3M to transcend the rigidity that often besets companies that become large and successful. As we will see in Chapter Five, many of these principles have been widely adopted by technology leaders to achieve boundaryless product development. For example, 3M:

- Encourages its people to meet with customers to understand their unmet needs and to stay ahead of them by developing solutions to these needs. For example, 3M makes light-reflective guide rails for highways. Although customers were satisfied with the product, 3M engineers decided that there were still too may accidents. By visiting technical experts throughout the company and through much trial and error, the scientists developed a light transmission technology that conveyed a beam of light for 500 feet along a rail. On European mountain roads where the new product is now used, accidents have declined dramatically.

- Allows its engineers and scientists to spend 15 percent of their time on any research project that interests them. This practice has resulted in very successful products, such as the $100 million "Post-It" note. When this practice is combined with an understanding of customers' unmet needs, it becomes a particularly powerful way to create valuable new businesses.

- Uses an internal "best practices" system and encourages people to share their knowledge. This element of 3M's culture is quite counterintuitive to many companies where knowledge is tightly guarded by each research team. By placing the emphasis on harnessing the company's expertise for the benefit of customers, 3M enjoys a powerful advantage over its more territorial peers.

- Measures the percentage of sales from new products. (3M has increased the standard from 25 percent to 30 percent of sales in its forty business units.) While this measure may have its flaws (as we will see in Chapter Eight), it does reinforce the importance of creating new products that add to revenues.

- Is honest about new product ideas that do not appear to be commercially viable. As we will see in Chapter Seven, this practice is an essential element of *disciplined* resource allocation. Because 3M enables the sponsors of canceled projects to try to find sponsors elsewhere in the company, 3M's intellectual honesty reinforces the respect that the company holds for its people.

- Holds annual celebrations for R&D, such as 3M's Oscar night, in which four eminent innovators are inducted into the Carlton

Society, to the cheers of their coworkers. This simple practice reinforces the pride that 3M employees take in innovation.

Microsoft

The process that Microsoft followed in the development of its server operating system, Windows NT, exemplifies its culture of starting from behind and taking over a market through persistence. Microsoft's DOS system lagged CP/M, Windows trailed Apple Lisa and Macintosh, Excel straggled behind Lotus 1-2-3, and Windows NT fought to overcome UNIX for over a decade. In the case of Windows, for example, version 1.0 failed, as did version 2.0. Version 3.0 was modestly successful. Finally, Windows 3.1 took off and became an outstanding success.

Windows NT appears poised to follow a similar pattern. As the *Wall Street Journal* (Clark, 1996) points out, from an unsuccessful introduction in 1993, Windows NT was rewritten several times, and by mid-1996 it controlled 19 percent of the market for server operating systems (as compared to 24 percent for UNIX and 42 percent for Novell). The introduction of Windows NT 4.0 in July 1996 appeared to represent the successful culmination of its $500 million development investment.

The Windows NT story illustrates the problems that a company can encounter when its products are developed in isolation from the customer. The story also shows how a company can salvage a failing product when it focuses its developers on improving the product to make customers happy.

The development effort for Windows NT 3.1 began in 1989 and took the four-hundred-person development team four years. The first version of the product, Windows NT 3.1, ran very slowly and consisted of 6.1 million lines of code.

Despite the less than stellar results, Jim Allchin, the executive who led this development effort, remained in charge of the product. Allchin realized that one of the key problems with the first version was that the development team had spent too much time away from customers. For example, because developers used computers that were much more powerful than the ones that typical NT customers used, they were not bothered that Windows NT required 24 megabytes of memory.

To save the product, Allchin created formal links between engineers and customers. Programmers handled technical support calls from customers and traveled to company sites where Windows NT was being used. Each time Windows NT won or lost a competitive bid from a big customer, sales staff e-mailed the news to each member of the development team.

Microsoft also sent betas of new versions of the program to thousands of customers. Then the company conducted telephone polls to find out whether all the bugs had been eliminated. Allchin also clipped bad reviews of Windows NT from trade publications and assigned team members to ensure that the program would be ranked number one in each category measured.

Furthermore, in response to customer complaints about the product's slow speed, Microsoft hired a sixteen-person team of programmers to design code to speed up sections of the program. These tactics led to a tremendous improvement in product performance. Although Windows NT 4.0 grew to 16.5 million lines of code, it ran up to eight times faster than the first version and used a third less memory. A server that formerly supported 150 users could now serve one thousand users with the same response time. And, compared to UNIX, Windows NT 4.0 had a very user-friendly interface and a significantly lower price ($2,000 less per computer).

As a result of these advantages, Windows NT sold four hundred and fifty thousand copies during the year ending June 30, 1996—three times the 1995 volume. Steve Ballmer, Microsoft's executive vice president, expected to ship approximately nine hundred thousand copies of the product in fiscal 1997.

Oracle

Oracle is a $3 billion database software and services company. Its return on equity exceeded 40 percent over the last five years. Larry Ellison, Oracle's chairman, has a personal net worth in excess of $6 billion.

Oracle is an intensely competitive company. In fact, at times it appears as though Oracle's chairman is engaged in a personal competition with Bill Gates. And this competitiveness permeates the company. Two anecdotes illustrate Oracle's competitiveness:

When Bill Gates announced that he was building a $30 million house in Bellevue, Washington, Ellison constructed a $40 million Japanese-style compound in Woodside, California. Ellison bought a T-38 supersonic jet fighter and jokingly told a *Forbes* reporter (Michaels, 1996, p. 16), "Maybe I should fire a few Maverick missiles in [Gates's] living room."

As Michael Hodos of Oracle Worldwide Technical Support said in Oracle's 1994 annual report, "We're an incredibly competitive company comprised of incredibly competitive people, and sometimes this competitiveness comes out in ways that make us smile. Last time we had a blood drive, I heard one donor suddenly shout to another in triumph, 'Beat you!' because she had managed to give her pint first!"

Although 3M, Microsoft, and Oracle have many differences in their business strategies and organizational styles, they share the common elements of a winning culture that is characteristic of top technology companies: they attract very talented people who take pride in winning and in working on products that have a positive impact on society; they encourage people to innovate in ways that create products and services that customers value; they promote internal competition and deal with failure in an honest and productive way; and they invest in people to ensure that they will be able to maintain their competitive advantage.

Top Team Players

Leading technology companies hire top team players and get them to work very long hours. CEOs of top technology companies use recruiting as a way to replicate themselves. They use common criteria for the scientists and engineers that they seek to attract and retain. The desired recruit has attended a leading school in the specific field of study; has graduated at the top of his or her class academically (from top 10 percent to top 1 percent) depending on the company and the school; has done research that is respected by experts in his or her field; demonstrates a deep personal interest in the field as evidenced by hobbies that are related to his or her research; has an ability and aptitude for learning outside his or her specific area of expertise; enjoys working as part of a team of people with different backgrounds and experience; and is highly competitive and takes pride in winning. The recruiting practices at HP, Cisco Systems, and Microsoft exemplify the importance of these attributes.

Hewlett-Packard

HP realized that it needed to approach on-campus recruiting in a very systematic fashion in order to fuel its growth, so the company targeted specific schools that it perceived to be in the top tier for the engineering and scientific disciplines for which it was hiring.

HP developed relationships with professors in specific departments. Through these relationships, HP hoped to make professors aware of the criteria they were using and to obtain names of students who met their criteria. The selection process was intended to identify students who were similar to the HP people doing the hiring. This process tested students' academic performance (top 10 percent of their classes), challenged their ability to solve technical problems on their feet, and examined the depth of their interest in their field as evidenced by their hobbies (for example, did they have a ham radio or a PC at home). Finally, HP's selection process assessed candidates' ability to work effectively with others (from May 10, 1996 interview with Dean Morton, HP's retired executive vice president, COO, and director).

Cisco Systems

Cisco Systems makes equipment that allows computer networks to communicate with each other. It is one of the most successful companies in American business. Between 1991 and 1995, for example, its return on equity averaged 56 percent, its revenues grew at an average annual rate of 83 percent, and its stock price increased 2,750 percent. Cisco Systems drew heavily on HP for ideas on how to organize as it grew.

Cisco has developed some creative ideas on how to recruit top people, as well. In an article in *Forbes* (Dolan, 1996), Cisco's CEO,

John Chambers, recounted the development of Cisco's highly effective "Friends" recruiting program. Cisco had learned from its engineers that people were not willing to switch jobs unless they knew someone who could provide a realistic picture of Cisco's work environment. In response to this feedback, Cisco started its Friends program to give potential employees an opportunity to "make a friend" at Cisco.

Cisco's Web home page includes a separate icon for the Friends program. Potential employees can click on the icon and select from open job listings. Their resumes can be attached or typed into the system. Cisco's corporate employment group can then match the resume with a volunteer Friend. This person then receives an e-mail message directing them to contact the potential employee within a day.

Cisco's Friends program has achieved excellent results. The number of Web site hits has grown from thirteen thousand to fifty-four thousand every seven weeks. Furthermore, the company is now hiring between one-third and one-half of the candidates interviewed as a result of using the Friends program. This is a significant improvement as Cisco hired only one-tenth of all interviewed candidates before the program was initiated.

Microsoft

Microsoft seeks to attract and retain smart people. One former Microsoft employee suggested that Bill Gates perceives recruiting as a way to deal with his own mortality. Simply stated, Gates looks for people like himself.

According to Gates, being "smart" means being able to understand and probe complex things quickly and creatively. Smart people have a certain sharpness and an ability to absorb new facts. In Gates's view, smart people can walk into a situation, have something explained to them, and immediately say, "Well, what about this?" They can ask an insightful question, absorb new information, remember, and relate to domains that at first may not seem connected; they possess a certain creativity that allows them to be effective (Cusumano and Selby, 1995).

Microsoft looks for smart people for development, testing, and product management positions primarily from forty top colleges and universities. Candidates who survive the on-campus screening are invited to Microsoft for four to six interviews with individuals in their functional area. Interviews test for general smartness, focusing on ambition, IQ, and technical expertise and business judgment, with IQ most important. In the interviews, Microsoft asks such general questions as estimating the volume of water flowing down the Mississippi River and the number of gas stations in the United States. Microsoft hires 2 to 3 percent of the people that it interviews (Cusumano and Selby).

Microsoft places such an emphasis on hiring smart people that it actually acquires companies just to get their people. For example, in 1986 Microsoft acquired a small operating system company, Dynamical Systems. This company was founded by Nathan Myhrvold, currently a Microsoft group vice president, who cowrote with Gates the 1995 best-seller *The Road Ahead.*

Myhrvold graduated from high school at age fourteen, from UCLA at nineteen with a bachelor's degree in mathematics and a master's degree in geophysics and space physics, and from Princeton at twenty-three, with a master's in mathematical economics and a Ph.D. in theoretical physics. Myhrvold also accepted a post-doctoral fellowship at Cambridge University to do research under Stephen Hawking. In the summer following his first year, he returned to the United States to work on a programming project with some Princeton colleagues. Myhrvold became president of what became a software company in Berkeley called Dynamical Systems.

During the course of acquiring Dynamical Systems, Gates lost interest in certain features of its operating system software that had originally attracted him. Nevertheless, Gates completed the deal. As it turned out, this group of hires rose to senior technical positions within Microsoft. As Randall Stross states in his book *The Microsoft Way* (1996), Gates's decision bore out the wisdom of "acquiring smarts in bulk."

The driving force behind the effort to build a team of top people is the urge to replicate the strengths of the CEO. Simply stated, people like Bill Gates have a limited amount of time during each day to take care of business. The only way that these people can take on more work is to build organizations that can bring the same level of intelligence, energy, and business judgment to that additional volume of work. As Geoffrey Yang of Institutional Venture Partners, a Silicon Valley venture capital firm, pointed out, a B opportunity with an A team produces an A company, while an A opportunity with a B team yields a B company (Geoffrey Yang, personal communication, July 31, 1996).

Decentralized Decision Making

Technology leaders that reach a certain size break themselves into smaller divisions. These smaller divisions are designed to be more responsive to changing customer needs and to aggressive competitors. Although HP originated the idea, other technology companies, such as Cisco Systems, have imitated it. Why is this important? In many startups, the founding entrepreneur stays on too long. The company has trouble because the founder can't manage its continued growth. As John Chambers pointed out (Nee, 1996), the first round of decentralization often requires a change in executive management. If this transition is managed smoothly, however, customers and shareholders benefit.

Although with decentralization companies run the risk of creating duplicative operations, particularly in such "back office" functions as finance, human resources, and the like, there are many advantages of decentralization for technology leaders.

• As already mentioned, smaller divisions can be more responsive to changes in customer needs, to strategies of aggressive competitors, and to "weak signals" that may portend technological paradigm shifts.

• Decentralized units have more direct control of all the resources required to compete effectively. These resources include functional specialists in engineering, manufacturing, marketing, and sales. And these smaller units enhance the ability of the CEO and the board of directors to see each division as a separate business for capital allocation purposes.

• The management and employees of the decentralized unit experience a greater feeling of ownership, motivation, and accountability for results; deeper "bench strength" results from the excellent management development opportunity provided to division managers.

Hewlett-Packard provided Cisco Systems with many of the ideas that it used to design its decentralized structure. 3Com, a Cisco competitor, is implementing a more radical form of decentralization. For each company, the purpose of the structure was to build new enterprises within the context of the larger organization.

Hewlett-Packard

HP empowered people from early in its history, believing that management should give employees a clear objective. Reflecting the company's respect for the individual, HP gave employees the freedom to achieve that objective. HP also realized that employees would only be willing to achieve management objectives if the organization recognized that individual's contribution (Collins and Porras, 1994).

As HP expanded in the 1950s, this management method was extended into a decentralized structure of autonomous divisions that were established as though they were small businesses. Divisions had wide control over their own R&D, production, and marketing strategies and had wide discretion in operating decisions.

When HP entered a new business, it established a new division that was charged with entering the new business and defining the product that it would build. These divisions were located in several states and received R&D funds based on their relative level of innovation. Facilities that began as manufacturing plants could only achieve full divisional status by creating an innovative new product and taking it to market (Collins and Porras).

Cisco Systems

A much younger technology company, Cisco Systems learned from HP's approach to decentralization. When the company was founded in 1984 by two Stanford employees, it operated rather informally. In 1986, the two founders left Stanford and began to run the company from their living rooms.

In 1988, Cisco hired John Morgridge. His job was to match the company's infrastructure to its technology. Morgridge built a functional structure consisting of engineering, marketing, manufacturing, and so on, with each department reporting to the CEO. By the early 1990s, the centralized management structure began to slow down decision making and make it more difficult for Cisco to sustain its 80 percent per year growth rates.

In 1995, John Chambers, Cisco's current CEO, created five business units that focused on specific technologies and common competitors. Chambers believes that the success of decentralization hinges on the ability of Cisco business unit executives to challenge each other while continuing to work together as a team. How well has Cisco's approach to decentralization worked? One measure is the relative sizes of Cisco and Bay Networks, the merger of two formerly independent competitors, Wellfleet and SynOptics. In 1994, these two companies were 10 percent larger than Cisco; by 1996, however, Cisco was 100 percent larger than Bay Networks (Nee, 1996).

3Com

3Com, a Cisco competitor, is pushing decentralization even closer to the individual employee. 3Com's organization structure is based on its analysis of the fundamental trends driving its business. CEO Eric Benhamou perceives that the rates of growth and change in its markets demand that industry participants renew themselves. (The following is from a personal interview with Eric Benhamou on May 19, 1996.)

3Com is taking four proactive measures to position itself to compete effectively for business in the networked society of the early twenty-first century. First, through iterative interaction with a number of people—including company executives, customers, and industry analysts—Benhamou is developing a vision or general framework for where 3Com needs to be in the future. Through this interaction, Benhamou has created a shared vision. Second, 3Com is creating local business units or product development teams that are market and technology oriented. Third, the company is creating a team of senior people in different functions and geographic regions who will be charged with developing a plan to implement the vision. Finally, the company will define the activities of its employees as they contribute to the achievement of the vision and make their contribution to society.

Within the context of a clearly articulated vision, employees will find quick and effective ways of choosing how they want to use their talents. They will form loose couplings with others both inside and outside of 3Com in order to achieve common objectives, such as developing new products, meeting the needs of a customer, or participating in events such as trade shows.

3Com's organization is less a pyramid than a Web page of hypertext links. This structure liberates people from the rigidity of the classic hierarchical organization. It encourages the right people to work together in the right place at the right time and then move on to the next project.

3Com will create a technology infrastructure to support this organization, providing financial, competitive, industry, and other information that people need to do their jobs. The company will make this information available to all employees in a variety of media.

Technology leaders don't allow organization structure to inhibit changes in strategy. So as they move into new businesses or out of old ones, technology leaders change the structure of their organizations. This is not unique to high-tech companies. What is instructive about technology leaders is that they excel at structuring their organizations to get the most out of very talented and ambitious people. And they are often more adept than their competitors at using technology to help people work together more effectively.

Entrepreneurial Incentives

Technology leaders recognize that without the right incentives, the other elements described in this chapter will not produce the results that management wants. If incentives are not aligned with these other elements, employees get cynical, which obviously can make it more difficult for them to achieve their full potential. Among peer companies, it is quite common to hear about individuals who develop new products that generate substantial revenues for their employers; when these individuals ask their supervisors how the company plans to reward their efforts on behalf of the company, the individuals are told that they can keep their jobs.

What incentives do technology leaders provide their employees? In many cases, they pay base salaries that are below their industry average. This enables technology leaders to keep their fixed costs relatively low. Often technology leaders offer bonuses that are linked to company performance. This performance may be measured in terms of financial results and customer satisfaction. And, depending on performance, employees may get a total cash compensation package that is higher than that of peer organizations.

In most cases, technology leaders offer their employees stock options, whose value has historically risen very quickly and which represent real opportunities to create personal wealth. However, the options become valuable only if the employees push themselves to develop a winning product that increases the value of the company.

Technology leaders recognize that top employees are motivated by three things: the personal satisfaction of working on products that make a difference to society, the intellectual stimulation of working with people that they respect, and a chance to generate personal wealth in the process. In order to provide these entrepreneurial incentives, technology leaders align employee objectives, performance measurement, career development, and financial incentives. Thermo Electron, Microsoft, and Cisco Systems have developed compensation systems that reflect these principles.

Thermo Electron Corporation

Thermo Electron is a technology company focused on environmental, energy, biomedical, and instrumentation markets worldwide. According to Thermo Electron's 1995 annual report, the company employs over twelve thousand people and generated revenues of $2.2 billion in 1995. At the end of 1995, the weighted average compound annual return since the initial public offering (IPO) dates for all fourteen of Thermo Electron's public subsidiaries was 33 percent.

At the core of these results is a "spinout" concept developed by Thermo Electron's chairman, George Hatsopolous, and his brother, John, who is CFO (Alster, 1995). A spinout involves taking public a minority interest in an operating unit run by a Thermo Electron engineer. The strategy was first implemented in 1983 as a way of providing a lower cost of capital for new businesses. Spinouts also have helped Thermo Electron to motivate and retain its best engineers as it has grown and diversified.

Although many companies, including IBM, Westinghouse, Kmart, and British Petroleum, have visited Thermo to learn about the strategy, these companies have not been able to replicate it. The more common *spinoff* strategy involves distributing to current shareholders a majority stake in a poorly performing business. By contrast, the spinout strategy involves selling a minority stake in a top performer to the public. Furthermore, with a spinoff, the proceeds of the equity sale are returned to the parent, whereas in a spinout, the cash goes to the operating unit. The challenge in replicating the spinout strategy is overcoming the CEO's fear of letting the most promising businesses go.

The spinout strategy has also fueled the entrepreneurial drive of Thermo Electron's best engineers. For example, Thermedics, Thermo's first IPO spinout, raised $6 million in 1983. At the time, Thermedics had no revenues, only a grant from the National Heart, Lung and Blood Institute (NHLBI) to develop an implantable heart-assist pump that Victor Poirier began developing in 1966. NHLBI's funding was evaporating and Poirier thought of leaving Thermo Electron. In taking the business public, however, Poirier became CEO and received options on twenty thousand Thermedics shares. Thermo Electron retained 86.6 percent of this jeopardized development project, valued at the time of the IPO at $40 million.

By 1989, the heart pump had not yet gained FDA approval. Meanwhile, Thermedics had developed a profitable new business in biomaterials and explosives detection. Because Poirier wanted to focus his efforts on the heart pump, Thermo spun the project out as Thermo Cardiosystems, selling a 40 percent stake to the public, giving Poirier $15 million in development capital for the pump, and valuing the project at $37 million, twenty-five times revenues.

Although the price appeared high at the time, Poirier's heart pump, which keeps the weak hearts of transplant patients pumping, was ultimately approved by the FDA. The market for the heart pumps consisted of fifty thousand patients awaiting the two thousand donor hearts that become available each year. Thermo Cardiosystems is anticipated to generate revenues of $100 million in 1997, and its shares rose from a split-adjusted January 1989 IPO price of $2.27 to $77.25 at the end of 1995, a compound annual return of 66 percent. Furthermore, Poirier's holdings in various Thermo companies totaled $5 million in January 1995 (Alster, 1995).

Thermo Electron provides legal, financial, and research support to its spun-out subsidiaries, but the greatest benefit of the spin-out strategy remains the entrepreneurial motivation it provides to its top engineers. As Dr. Hatsopolous has demonstrated repeatedly, rewarding a creative employee with $500,000 in stock options sets a powerful example for his or her colleagues (Wilke, 1993).

Microsoft

Microsoft's compensation approach is designed to maintain its 25 percent net margins while increasing its revenues, profits, and stock price. Its approach to compensation, which by 1995 had helped produce roughly 3,000 millionaires among its 17,800 employees, is an intrinsic element of the following "success cycle" (Cusumano and Selby, 1995):

• Microsoft grants stock options to attract the most talented and creative people in the industry. Microsoft pays a base salary below the industry average, thereby helping to preserve its net margins. Employees can exercise 25 percent of their stock options after working at Microsoft for eighteen months, and another 12.5 percent every six months thereafter. Employees can also put up to 10 percent of their salaries into stock purchases at 85 percent of market value.

• These talented and creative people, recognizing that their ability to achieve wealth through Microsoft stock appreciation is contingent on producing superior products, work fourteen-hour days and on weekends to meet aggressive project deadlines. If a deadline appears to be slipping on an important project, outside contractors are hired to help avert the slippage, thus adding resources without increasing fixed costs.

• Microsoft introduces superior products to the market, thereby contributing to Microsoft's sales growth, 25 percent of which goes to the bottom line.

• Microsoft's stock price rises substantially, allowing the employees with stock options (many of whom have been exhausted by their efforts) to resign with a substantial financial cushion.

• Microsoft's reputation for producing superior products and making its employees wealthy is reinforced, thus attracting a new group of young, talented programmers to the company.

Cisco Systems

Cisco uses three simple, effective compensation policies that few of its competitors replicate (Nee, 1996). These policies reflect fundamental Cisco Systems values: customer satisfaction, teamwork, and employee empowerment. The company's compensation policies reflect an understanding of the important interdependence of these values:

• In order to lead the industry, Cisco must listen to its customers and develop products that satisfy their needs. The company hires an independent party to conduct an annual customer satisfaction survey. Every person's bonus, from the president to the individual manager, depends on the results of this survey. If the results have improved over the prior year, people receive a bonus. If the results have gone down, they do not receive their bonus or money is taken away from them.

• In order to satisfy customer internetworking needs, the different parts of Cisco's organization must work together effectively. The company ties compensation to team success, not individual success. John Chambers, Cisco's CEO, rewards leaders both on their results and on the quality of the teams they build. This practice is not common in Silicon Valley, where CEOs often let their management teams fight among themselves.

• To achieve effective teamwork, individuals must be empowered to do what they believe to be in the best interests of the company and themselves. Cisco Systems provides every employee with stock options from their first day of employment. This practice differs from other technology companies, which often wait six to twelve months before granting stock options to a subset of their employees. By providing these options, whose value appreciated quite dramatically between 1990 and 1995, Cisco creates a powerful financial incentive to work hard and effectively to make the company more valuable (John Morgridge, personal communication, June 14, 1996).

Of course, some technology companies are able to recruit employees who are seeking some balance between their business and personal lives. For example, Whitetree, a small Palo Alto, California-based internetworking equipment company, faces a tough recruiting climate in Silicon Valley. Larger companies tend to pay very high cash salaries that Whitetree cannot and does not want to pay.

Whitetree has found that it can attract smart people by offering fair compensation and by providing a really good work environment. As with many technology leaders, employees are the best recruiters. Whitetree is very flexible about work hours and location. The company believes that smart, motivated people produce. For example, one of its top hardware designers lives outside of California and visits as required. A high percentage of employees have ISDN (very high speed) access into Whitetree's corporate network. They can thus work flexibly during the week and over the weekend and avoid the California commute. Whitetree also employs a number of parents who need flexible work hours to manage their child care and to participate in some of their children's school activities.

Whitetree's compensation scheme values functional competence and teamwork. The review of any employee rated "exceptional" is discussed at the CEO's staff meeting. Lawrence wants the entire organization to be able to say "this person is really a top performer" (e-mail message from Maureen Lawrence, Whitetree CEO, December 4, 1996).

CEO Change Agenda

Many of the management approaches presented in this chapter originate with the CEO. To the extent that incumbent CEOs can adapt their leadership styles, corporate cultures, hiring practices, organization structure, and compensation systems, there are opportunities to benefit from the best practices that have been described. Because of the fundamental change that must occur to achieve the benefits described here, CEOs may consider the following action steps:

Recognize the need for change. An awareness of best practices could make the CEO feel uncomfortable about the company's relative position, but this discomfort could be the "weak signal" that initiates a change process. On the other extreme, a board member of a company in financial or competitive distress could simply decide to replace the CEO with a leader like the ones described in this chapter.

Build a case for action. A case for action must be based on facts. The Innovation Scorecard, described in detail in Chapter Eight, provides a framework for self-assessment. It provides a way to pinpoint the most fruitful areas for improvement. A case for action, however, must take into account an assessment of the company relative not only to its peers but also to changes in industry structure. These facts must be synthesized into a compelling case for change that the CEO can use to lead the organization.

Empower a team to develop strategic options. The CEO must use the case for action to recruit this team, which may consist of both internal and external resources for developing strategic options. These options may include many dimensions of choice, such as changing executive team members; corporate mission, values, and culture; organization structure; and recruiting, training, performance evaluation, and compensation policies. The team should discuss the various options and select the preferred strategy.

Develop and follow an implementation plan that begins with "short-term wins" to create momentum. Once the team has selected the strategy, it should create an implementation plan. To generate the organizational momentum needed to make the change stick, the plan should start with some short-term wins that will help people overcome their fear of change. For example, if a new bonus system tied to customer satisfaction in a high-performing division was installed successfully, this short-term win could motivate other divisions to learn from the first division's positive experience.

———⊗⊗⊗⊙———

Chapter Three describes the second key source of advantage that drives return on innovation: open technology. As we will see, technology leaders view technology as a way to meet customer needs. The key is to get the technology to the customer before the competition can get a foothold. If this means buying a company or licensing the technology, technology leaders are often happy to do it. If the technology can be obtained faster by developing it internally, technology leaders will do so.

Chapter Three

Open Technology I
Managing the Core

Technology leaders build their wealth on a foundation of core technologies. If the core technologies can generate products that are uniquely valuable to customers, this foundation is strong. However, the value of a firm's core technologies can often erode if paradigm-shifting technologies reduce the firm's ability to create products that customers value. This issue has tripped up some of the best technology companies because they have a very hard time "cannibalizing" themselves. Conversely, because technology leaders take advantage of these paradigm shifts, they are very hard for competitors to stop.

To survive, technology companies must manage their core technologies in response to the technologies' relative value to customers. As the value of a technology increases relative to competing technologies, the firm must invest. When the technology begins to stagnate, the firm must cannibalize it either through internal development or through partnerships.

For example, Intel has built its entire business around the idea of competing with itself more aggressively than with its external competitors. Intel's chairman, Gordon Moore, plotted the price and performance of successive generations of microprocessors. He discovered that the power and complexity of silicon chips doubled every twelve months, a figure that he later extended to eighteen months (Lenzner, 1995), with proportional decreases in cost.

Intel has repeated a cycle of success that is, in some respects, atypical of the success cycles used by other technology companies. By 1996, Intel had built a $16 billion business with a market capitalization of $62 billion by being the first in its industry to introduce the microprocessor that achieves the next doubling in performance. Intel is atypical because it makes substantial investments in semiconductor fabrication facilities ("fabs"), which currently cost in excess of $1 billion, based on its forecast of what customer performance requirements will be when its next product is introduced in two to three years. By beating its competitors to market with the next generation, Intel grabs the lion's share of the market, maximizes the utilization of its fabs, achieves economies of scale, and refills its coffers for investment in the next product cycle (Crockett, 1996).

Interestingly, Intel has created operating units, such as the embedded-systems business, that are intended to sell its now "obsolete" CPUs to the non-PC CPU market. By selling its earlier generations of CPUs to such segments as data communications, factory automation, laser printers, and other non-PC segments, Intel keeps these fully depreciated fabs utilized, generating positive cash flow that is also plowed back into the next generation of chips. As the cost of building a fab increases to an estimated $2.5 billion by 1997 and $10 billion by 2000, it is likely that few competitors will remain who can keep the pace of Intel's success cycle.

Intel's success at leading the pack creates interesting dangers as well. For example, Intel is now trying to use its dominance in the CPU market to incorporate the functionality of other chips on the motherboard into its CPUs. Although this new chip has the potential to create more customer value, it also runs the risk of reinforcing a "product-centric," not "customer-centric," mentality that could ultimately put Intel in a position where it produces chips that customers don't want. The economic cycle thus can be sustained only if software and computer makers keep coming up with machines that consumers keep buying. Furthermore, the intense pressure that Intel's success cycle places on its people, particularly its fab managers, has the potential to burn out Intel's best people, leaving weaknesses in its middle management ranks.

For executives in technology companies, the success and challenges of companies like Intel have important implications for how they manage their core technologies. Management techniques include the following: (1) explicitly identifying core technologies; (2) objectively valuing core technologies; (3) identifying "leverage-point technologies" and forging them into industry standards; (4) monitoring new technologies that could complement or undermine the firm's core technology portfolio; and (5) creating partnerships or making acquisitions (or both) to gain access to the full set of technologies or capabilities the firm needs to meet the changing needs and purchasing behavior of its customers.

What are core technologies? Core technologies are specific areas of technical expertise (including people, patents, and other intellectual property) that enable a firm to develop products. In order to be "core," these technologies must meet three criteria: (1) they must create customer value, (2) they must be applicable to a wide range of markets, and (3) they must be competitively unique and difficult to copy.

As we will explore later in this chapter, core technologies must often be complemented by other capabilities in order to create a successful business. This situation occurs quite frequently in the biotechnology and medical products industries: a scientist might develop promising research but the company might lack the manufacturing and distribution capabilities to turn this research into a viable business.

This chapter explores the five techniques that technology leaders use to manage their core technologies. For each step in the process, we will look at and extract principles from specific examples. The chapter concludes with a description of the steps that CEOs can take to adopt the most relevant of these principles into their own organizations.

Identify Core Technologies

Before a firm can manage its core technologies, it must first identify them, as have technology leaders Hewlett-Packard and Merck.

Hewlett-Packard

HP developed a list of past contributions and current research areas that includes five broad technologies, with specific product categories that these technologies helped to spawn. For example, the analytical technology category helped create a range of chemical analysis products. Analytical products include the UV/Visible

Spectrometer, Chemical Experts for IR Spectra, and Capillary Electrophoresis ("HP Labs," 1995).

The spawning of these new products resulted from HP's famed "management by walking around" (MBWA) process. Researchers within the HP labs would build prototypes of products that reflected their progress within specific technical areas. Engineers from the operating divisions would visit the labs and examine the prototypes. If the operating divisions liked what they saw, they would adopt them as a product.

Because the customers of the products in the analytical area were also scientists, in this case analytical chemists, the process worked effectively. As we will see in Chapter Six, this approach can be dangerous if the customer is a consumer, not a scientist.

Merck

Merck organized its research laboratories around its core technologies, which Merck calls its "centers of excellence." Each center is run by a vice president who reports to the executive vice president of science and technology. Merck has six core technologies represented by research laboratories throughout the world. These technologies include respiratory and allergy; neuroscience; safety assessment; antiviral, cancer, and infectious disease; cardiovascular; and antibiotic screening (from Merck corporate literature, May 1995).

At Merck, the technology helps determine which research projects get funded. If there is a large unmet need and Merck scientists have an edge in the science to treat the disease, then people in that research lab will be assigned to the project. The pattern of resource allocation to the research labs is a good reflection of what Merck perceives to be its core technologies.

———— ∞∞∞ ————

Although many peer companies have participated in the "exercise" of identifying their core technologies, what differentiates technology leaders from their peers is what they do once they have identified their core technologies. Technology leaders constantly monitor their core technologies to see whether they still meet the three criteria outlined earlier.

Peer companies tend to take a more cautious approach. They prefer to wait until there is very strong external evidence of a problem with the current core technology before they begin the search for a substitute. Peer companies are more concerned about protecting the past than about investing for the future.

Value Core Technologies

The next step in managing core technologies is to value them. Although technology leaders approach this valuation process in a systematic fashion, and the outcome may be quantitative, the process remains quite subjective. The starting point for assigning values to core technologies is to make a comprehensive list of the current and possible market segments in which potential products could be sold. Once you have developed a list of market segments, you can estimate the value of the core technology, based on explicit assumptions about market unit volume and growth rate, product pricing and profit margins, market share, and competitive response. These assumptions are subjective, with uncertainty resulting from management's outlook and the stage of development of these markets. The theoretical basis for the valuation of core technologies is the net present value of the cash flows generated by the products that the technologies spawn.

The process by which Microsoft licensed MS-DOS to IBM for its PC operating system illustrates the important role that differences in management perspective play in valuing core technologies. IBM approached Microsoft in 1981 to provide an operating system for its to-be-developed personal computer (PC). IBM had assumed, incorrectly, that Microsoft had already developed a personal computer operating system because the company had developed BASIC and other programming languages for other personal computers. Microsoft did tell IBM that it felt that it could develop an operating system for the PC fairly quickly.

Microsoft found a struggling software company in the Seattle area, Seattle Computer, that had developed a prototype for a 16-bit Intel operating system. Microsoft licensed the product, Q-DOS (Quick and Dirty Operating System), for $75,000. IBM licensed

DOS, a modified version of Q-DOS, from Microsoft for an up-front payment of $150,000 and no royalties. IBM, incorrectly assuming that no "plug-compatible" market would emerge to compete with its PC, ceded to Microsoft all the rights to license MS-DOS to makers of PC-compatible computers.

Bill Gates assumed, correctly, that a PC-compatible market would emerge soon after IBM began selling its PC. In fact, such companies as Compaq, Dell, Packard Bell, AST Research, and many others built up substantial market positions, overtaking IBM. By bundling its operating system with the PC-compatible hardware, charging a nominal royalty, Microsoft established its operating system as the industry standard—creating the foundation for its subsequent success (Cusumano and Selby, 1995). Larry Ellison, Oracle's CEO, has suggested that IBM had made the most expensive mistake in business history, costing it $100 billion: the combined market capitalization of Microsoft and Intel at the time of his comment. (Stephens, 1996).

As this example demonstrates, the value of core technology depends on who is valuing it. This example also reinforces the importance of accurate, objective valuations. Although it is unlikely that Microsoft was able to estimate the precise value that would be created by licensing MS-DOS to vendors of PC-compatible computers, the fact that Gates anticipated that this market would emerge and become valuable, while IBM assumed that it would be insignificant, was a difference in valuation assumptions that in retrospect had tremendous economic significance. It appears that IBM's mistake was not that it licensed the technology from Microsoft but that it failed to take advantage of the huge market opportunity that this licensing decision helped create.

Focus on Leverage-Point Technologies

Having valued their core technologies, technology leaders take strategic action to enhance their value. One essential way to do this is to focus on "leverage-point technologies" and make them industry standards. Microsoft and other leading technology companies have recognized that certain technologies within a system can become the leverage point for organizing the development efforts of third parties. Examples of leverage-point technologies include the operating system, the CPU, and the relational database.

By being perceived as the industry leader in a specific leverage-point technology, a company can offer third parties the security that the system in which they are investing resources has the greatest potential to become the industry standard. If the system does become the industry standard, the owner of the leverage-point technology and the third parties are likely to earn a high return on their investment. This outcome is based on an assumption, frequently born out, that the mass market will buy the system that is considered the industry standard. Conversely, if the system does not become the industry standard, all participants are likely to be hurt.

Cisco Systems and Compaq offer interesting perspectives on how to pinpoint these leverage-point technologies and then establish themselves as the industry standard.

Cisco Systems

Cisco Systems hardware and software products are used to link computers so that people have access to information—regardless of differences in time, place, or computer system. A critical element in Cisco's success has been its ability to establish its operating system as the industry standard. For example, this standard has enabled Cisco to control over 80 percent of the market for Internet routers (a kind of traffic cop for data). The Cisco Internetwork Operating System (IOS) enables customers to connect networks that are physically far apart. IOS also enables customers to move from one network type to another without having to spend a lot of money. IOS supports over sixteen standard ways for computers to send and receive data, known as network protocols.

IOS supports users throughout a company, giving them what they have told Cisco that they need. It offers security and data integrity, controls and unifies distributed network intelligence, and enables customers to add new services, features, and applications to the internetwork.

Cisco has been able to offer these benefits to customers because it formed a partnership with other industry participants including Cabletron Systems and Bay Networks. This partnership ensured that each technology partner included Cisco's operating system on their products. By creating this industry standard, Cisco and its partners benefit by meeting the customer need for different makes of equipment to work together in the rapidly growing internetworking industry. The integrated solution increases sales for all participants. Customers protect their investments while enjoying a flexible path for meeting demand growth and responding to changes in the type of information that their networks need to handle (interview with John Morgridge, June 14, 1996).

Another important contributor to Cisco's market leadership is the company's method of managing manufacturing. In particular, Cisco maintains a high-quality process, outsources noncore activities, and tailors hardware and software to meet the specific needs of its customers. The company's manufacturing processes are ISO 9001–certified. To increase speed and flexibility, the company subcontracts printed circuit board assembly, in-circuit test, and product repair. Cisco also shortens time-to-market by installing its proprietary software on electronically programmable memory chips. This manufacturing process enables the company to build hardware and software configurations that meet individual customer requirements. Cisco's strength in manufacturing results in a very low level of customer returns and helps persuade customers that Cisco is the industry leader.

The Cisco example illustrates several important principles regarding the focus on leverage-point technologies:

Leverage-point technologies must create customer value. Cisco recognized that in order to enable customers to implement true interoperability, its operating system would need to work with competing products and be easy to modify to accommodate new internetworking products.

Leverage-point technologies must be managed to enlist third-party participation. Cisco developed and implemented a management approach that enlisted the support of third parties. Cisco created economic incentives that motivated competitors and other third parties to support the development of Cisco's operating system as the industry standard.

Leverage-point technologies must be supported by excellent product supply capabilities. Although owning the industry-standard operating system was a critical element for Cisco's success, it was not sufficient. Cisco developed manufacturing, distribution, and support capabilities that reinforced the customer perception that Cisco's brand is a standard of excellence.

Compaq Computer

Compaq, a $15 billion market leader in desktop and portable PCs and servers, established an industry standard in desktop computers. Compaq integrated system components to meet customer needs for the highest levels of performance and quality at a competitive total ownership cost. By creating products with superior performance and quality, a 1995 survey indicated that business customers were willing to pay a $318 premium for Compaq products (from Compaq's 1995 annual report).

Compaq was the leading vendor of desktop PCs worldwide in 1994 and 1995 with 10 percent market share, representing shipments of almost six million units, outselling its nearest competitor by one million PCs and almost two market share points. Compaq also built a dominant position in the worldwide PC server and superserver market, leading IBM and HP by wide margins between 1992 and 1995, and controlling 36 percent of the market compared to 14 percent for IBM and 12 percent for HP in 1995 (from Compaq's 1995 annual report).

As a result of its leadership in the server market, Compaq has become the industry-standard platform for development partners such as Microsoft, Oracle, Novell, and SAP. For example, Lyondell Petrochemical, a leading U.S. petrochemical producer, chose a partnership between SAP America, Compaq, and Microsoft to implement a new client-server computing platform. This platform was designed to enable Lyondell customers to access product pricing and availability information and to place orders electronically. Lyondell's director of information services chose the alliance because the company was looking for the best mix of technological leaders that could work together.

How did Compaq achieve this success? According to Compaq's 1994 annual report, Compaq has consistently lowered its prices while expanding its product functionality. Between 1993 and 1994, for example, Compaq created customer value while increasing its net income by almost 90 percent. The key to Compaq's ability to increase profitability while lowering prices is economies of scale. Compaq increased its unit volumes while consciously managing its cost and quality through manufacturing process redesign. Compaq invested in more manufacturing capacity in five locations and redesigned its products so that they could be manufactured in half the time. Compaq also increased by 25 percent the number of PCs built per square foot of factory space. As a result, labor and overhead costs dropped 19 percent between 1993 and 1994, and sales per employee rose to $872,000—roughly 40 percent higher than Compaq's closest competitor. While Compaq was increasing its productivity, it was also integrating the functionality of a telephone, answering machine, TV, fax/modem, CD-ROM, and stereo in a single device.

Between 1985 and 1995, the power of Compaq's desktop machines increased over 12,000 percent while their price dropped 30 percent. This improvement in the price-performance ratio, coupled with high quality and reliability, are key contributors to the power of the Compaq brand. Compaq's success between 1984 and 1994 is best measured by the 43 percent average annual rate of return in its stock (nine times the S&P 500 rate), representing an increase in Compaq's market capitalization from $173 million to $10.3 billion.

The Compaq example illustrates several important principles. First, the company that takes the lead in developing leverage-point technologies into the industry standard ends up with the largest market share.

Second, to achieve that leadership position, companies must truly listen to customers. To be a leader, companies must understand how customer needs can be translated into product attributes that, when taken together, are perceived to be the safest bet in the industry. This is critically important because customers and third parties often allocate resources—either to buy the product or to develop a new product to support the platform—before there is any certainty regarding whether the platform will become the industry standard.

Third, because in most cases leverage-point technologies constitute only one component of the complete customer solution, companies must recruit and work together with partners who lead in other leverage-point technologies and who can fill in the missing pieces.

Fourth, efficient, high-quality manufacturing procedures often combine with engineering talent to deliver the consistently high levels of customer value that enable companies to create the industry standard.

Finally, although companies like Compaq may have patents on their products and processes (Compaq has 275 U.S. patents and 300 pending), the economic benefits that Compaq has enjoyed and that are traditionally associated with patents, particularly in the pharmaceutical industry, did not result from the patent protection. For Compaq and other information technology leaders, the growth in market value and earnings were due, in large part, to their ability to become the standard and dominate the markets in which they participate.

Monitor New Technologies

One of the most common sources of corporate failure is the inability to adapt to a new technological paradigm. The buggy whip industry was decimated by automobiles, the vacuum tube industry contracted as a result of the transistor, and the transistor business was largely replaced by the semiconductor industry. Many of the technology leaders in this book have incorporated an understanding of this pattern into their management processes.

For example, Synopsys's CEO, Aart de Geus, points out that in order for technology companies to survive, they must achieve market dominance in each successive wave of technology (Aart de Geus, personal communication, August 28, 1996). In order to achieve this dominance, companies need to identify where the next exponential, or 10x, technology change will occur. Companies must risk significant capital and human resources on this next wave, before it is clear that customers will embrace the next generation.

Whether any individual firm can continue to adapt to changing technologies remains to be seen. However, many technology leaders have demonstrated the ability to jump the curve from one technology paradigm to the next.

Companies like HP, Johnson & Johnson, and Merck have demonstrated the ability to scan for new technologies that could either complement or completely undermine their traditional business models. This scanning capability is usually staffed by individuals with a deep knowledge of the company's technologies. These individuals also have a broad network of contacts in organizations outside the company that have been, and are anticipated to be, sources of innovative technologies. The strategies for dealing with these innovations may include forming partnerships, acquiring, or acting as a source of operating capital. These leading firms share an ability to recognize the limitations of their traditional business model, to see where that model could be vulnerable, and to form business relationships that enable them to profit from technological paradigm shifts instead of being harmed by them.

Hewlett-Packard

HP capitalized on its internally developed inkjet technology to take PC printer market leadership from Epson, the dominant dot matrix printer vendor. This story illustrates how HP transformed its entire approach to product development; it demonstrates the transformation of HPs next bench culture into a team approach in which HP engineers learned to understand customers and competitors—and in so doing, built a huge new business. According to the *Wall Street Journal* (Yoder, 1994), between 1988 and 1995, overall inkjet unit volume rose from zero to an estimated eight million units while dot matrix unit volume dropped from six million to three million units.

An HP engineer discovered inkjet printing in 1979 while working in a converted janitor's closet in HP's Vancouver, Washington, office. He was charging a thin metal film with electricity; when the metal grew hot, liquid trapped underneath began to boil and spurted out, splattering drops of liquid over his lab bench. This discovery evolved into the "thermal" inkjet. HP's executive in charge, Richard Hackborn, recognized that inkjet technology had several advantages over laser printers for the mass market: it was less expensive, more easily adaptable for color printing, and had not been perfected by competitors.

HP's first inkjet printer, introduced in 1984, was not a success. It required special paper and it printed only ninety-six dots per inch (compared with six hundred dots in 1995). Whereas Epson, a vendor of dot matrix printers, thought that HP's first product was an embarrassment, HP saw inkjet technology as the basis for satisfying a mass market that would demand higher-quality printouts of text, graphics, and photographs. Hackborn chose to "learn from the Japanese" by investing heavily in its low-cost inkjet technology, building it into a family of products that could fill retail shelves.

Canon, which had patented early inkjet designs and then shared them with HP, chose a complex implementation that would take many years to develop. Epson's U.S. executives tried unsuccessfully to convince Japanese headquarters that Epson should introduce a high-quality printer to meet the demands of low-budget U.S. PC users. Because of Epson's large dot matrix revenue base, profits, and technological history, Epson declined to develop its expensive inkjet technology variant.

Meanwhile, HP engineers filed several patents on its own inkjet technology and began a process of continual improvement to solve the inkjet's problems. HP developed print heads that could generate three hundred dots per inch and made inks that would stay liquid in the cartridge but dry instantly on plain paper.

In 1988, HP introduced the Deskjet, the first version of the plain-paper copier that ultimately took share from the Japanese products. Although HP had no inkjet rivals at the time, the product was not meeting its sales goals in 1989. The inkjet was competing with HP's more costly laser printers. Inkjet sales were too low to support its high research and manufacturing costs. Due to HP's policy of requiring its divisions to be financially self-supporting, the inkjet division needed new markets to avert a financial crisis.

In fall 1989, a group of engineers and managers held a two-day retreat at Mount Hood. While reviewing market share charts, HP realized that it had been targeting the wrong enemy. Instead of positioning the inkjet as a low-cost alternative to HP's laser printers, the managers decided to attack the Japanese-dominated dot matrix market. Dot matrix had poor print quality and color. Furthermore, Epson, the dot matrix leader, had no competitive inkjet and was distracted by an expensive and failing effort to sell a PC.

HP attacked Epson beginning with an in-depth analysis of Epson's market share, marketing strategies, public financial data, loyal customers, and top managers. In addition, HP engineers reverse-engineered Epson printers to search for design and manufacturing ideas. HP's analysis of Epson generated useful insights. HP discovered that Epson marketers convinced stores to put printers in the most prominent locations. Epson used price cuts to defend itself from challengers. Consumers liked Epson reliability.

Finally, HP found out that Epson printers were designed to be easy to manufacture.

HP responded by demanding that stores put its printers next to Epson's. HP tripled its warranty and redesigned its printers for ease of manufacturing. In its competitor analysis, HP had also learned that Epson could create a very broad product line by making slight variations in the same basic platform. HP, on the other hand, had a history of creating an entirely new platform for each new product version.

Engineers were very upset at the suggestion to make minor modifications to the existing platform. They reluctantly agreed, however, after the product manager forced engineers to conduct a telephone poll of customers that revealed that customers wanted to buy a product that was a slight variation of HP's existing platform. By remaining with this platform, HP was able to introduce a product to market far earlier than its competitors for the now rapidly growing color printer market.

When Tandy opened its stores in 1991, it told suppliers to make inkjets available to meet what it anticipated to be very strong demand. Only HP had a product available. When Japanese printer makers that had been investing in inkjet research tried to enter the market, they found that HP had locked up many important patents. Citizen Watch Company, for example, found that HP had fifty patents covering how ink travels through the head. At NEC, years went by during which the company was unable to replicate HP's technology, enabling HP to gain an even greater lead over its competitors.

By the time Canon introduced the first credible competition, HP had already sold millions of its printers and had thousands of outlets for its replacement cartridges. HP used its experience to make continuous improvements in manufacturing. As a result, by 1994 the Deskjet cost half its 1988 price in constant dollars. When Canon was about to introduce a color inkjet printer in 1993, HP cut the price of its own version before Canon reached the market. The monochrome printer, priced at $995 in 1988, listed for $365 in 1994. When NEC tried to introduce an inexpensive monochrome inkjet printer, HP launched an improved color version and cut the price of its best-selling monochrome model by 40 percent over six months.

HP's willingness to compete with its earlier versions enabled it to increase revenues and dominate increasingly value-conscious segments of its market while blocking the entry of new competitors. Between 1984 and 1994, for example, HP's share of the U.S. printer market grew from 2 percent to 55 percent (Yoder, 1994).

The HP example illustrates several important elements of monitoring new technologies:

New technologies are often widely disseminated throughout an industry well in advance of any effort to commercialize them. In the case of inkjet, Canon and other competitors had access to the technology but chose not to develop it.

Barriers to implementing new technologies exist largely in the minds of industry participants. Canon and Epson, for example, viewed the past as a prologue for the future. They assumed that their prior success with other technologies would ensure their future success. HP had also developed a laser printer but decided to position its inkjet against dot matrix. HP's aggressive positioning against Canon and Epson contributed to HP's success.

Johnson & Johnson

Johnson & Johnson (J&J) implicitly recognizes that its own R&D staff cannot be relied on to develop paradigm-shifting technologies, so J&J has created an organization that is focused on licensing-in promising technologies from entrepreneurs and universities. The individuals who staff this licensing-in organization are in fact competing with other large companies for these licensing opportunities. J&J attempts to differentiate itself in this competition by assigning individuals who recognize that an alliance with a large company like J&J is often much more important to the startup than it is to the large company. In order to win the competition for licensing-in the best technologies, J&J has organized itself to share in the entrepreneur's sense of urgency and quick decision making.

For example, several years ago, J&J's Ethicon division licensed-in a stent developed by two surgeons. A stent is a device that props open blood vessels after cholesterol-clogged vessels have been opened using methods such as balloon angioplasty. By combining the compelling advantages of the technology with J&J's manufacturing and distribution capabilities, the stent grew quickly into a multimillion-dollar business for J&J. Furthermore, because the stent filled a gap in J&J's cardiovascular product strategy, J&J was willing to pay a higher price than another buyer might have paid for the stent business alone (from an interview with Alan Levy, CEO of Heartstream, May 15, 1996).

Merck

Merck is an interesting example of a technology leader that monitored changes, not only in technology but, more important, in the underlying structure of its industry. Prior to the late 1980s, Merck enjoyed the ability to raise pharmaceutical prices to cover its growing research and other expenditures. Merck was jolted during the late 1980s and early 1990s, however, as the bargaining power of payers (for example, governments, managed care groups, insurance companies, and employees) increased dramatically (Tanouye, 1996).

A new strategic group, pharmacy benefit management (PBM) companies, emerged to exploit this change in industry structure by inserting themselves between the pharmaceutical companies and the payers. PBMs are hired by health plans, for example, to manage their members' prescription costs. They reduce buyer purchasing and administrative costs by offering claims processing, discounts, and mail service. They review drug utilization to ensure that payers are offering the least-expensive drug that treats the patient's disease. They even offer "total disease management," a practice that forces pharmaceutical companies to demonstrate the cost effectiveness of their products relative to alternative means of treatment, measured by healthier patients and lower overall health care costs (Tanouye, 1996).

Merck was stunned by the power and rapid growth of these PBMs and feared that the power of PBMs to negotiate huge discounts from pharmaceutical companies would lead to a downward spiral in revenues. In response (according to Merck's 1994 annual report), Merck acquired the leading PBM company, Medco Containment Services, in November 1993 for $6.6 billion. Merck perceived that it could change the basis of competition in the industry by combining Merck's superior products and clinical expertise with

Medco's managed-care capabilities, technology, and drug utilization data.

Specifically, Merck would transfer to Medco its ability to generate data that show how patients react to drug treatments. In the short term, Medco would transfer to Merck its ability to cut drug and treatment costs for payers. In the longer term, Medco would provide its expertise in developing programs to create the healthiest patients at the lowest cost.

The results for Merck have been good. Prescriptions for Merck's drugs increased 20 percent across all PBMs in the first half of 1996 when compared with the previous six months. According to IMS America, a drug sales reporting firm, Merck's prescriptions through Medco grew by 30 percent. Although the results have been good, Medco's president, G. H. Lofberg, continues to perceive that the biggest payoff will come from the development of disease management programs (Tanouye, 1996).

---∞∞∞---

The J&J and Merck examples illustrate important differences between these technology leaders and their peers:

Technology leaders monitor changes in technology and in their industries. More important, they make significant resource commitments in response to these changes. This attitude contrasts with peer companies that demonstrate a tendency to ignore fundamental changes until it is too late for them to take action.

Technology leaders are good at bundling capabilities. They look at what is needed to create value for their customer base. If they don't have what their customers need, they partner or acquire to close the gap. As J&J demonstrates, it is important to adapt a big company culture to the demands of small companies that own a critical piece of the puzzle.

Partner or Acquire to Close the Capability Gap

Technology leaders pay close attention to changing customer needs and purchasing behavior. They compare their current technologies and capabilities with those required to satisfy their customers. If they lack the full set of capabilities, technology leaders take action, forming strategic alliances and acquiring companies that will enable them to offer the full bundle of capabilities that customers require.

Peer companies, on the other hand, have traditionally looked to develop all their technologies inside. Due in part to the primacy of engineering in these peer companies, it is a point of pride within their culture that their engineers invent every technology themselves.

This approach has many negative consequences. Companies that pursue this "not invented here" approach arrive too late to market with a technology that does not meet a real customer need. They lose market share to a competitor that has moved more aggressively to provide the best customer solution. And they waste financial and human resources by developing a technology that fails in the marketplace.

Microsoft and Cisco Systems are two technology leaders that have formed and managed strategic partnerships to fill capability gaps.

Microsoft

In the early 1990s, Microsoft began to perceive a potential threat from the Internet. The company had made money in the past by selling operating systems and application software to desktop PC users, a business model that could have been made irrelevant depending on how the Internet evolved as a business.

In response to this perceived threat, Microsoft formed a broad array of strategic partnerships that were designed to give Microsoft flexibility in light of the uncertain future of the Internet. As executive vice president Steve Ballmer pointed out, Microsoft does not want to be in a position of being caught unprepared should a new technology emerge that makes its technology obsolete (Cusumano and Selby, 1995). Microsoft's move into this business was not motivated primarily by fear, however. Bill Gates had estimated that the market's shopping and advertising categories alone could reach $100 billion. The head of on-line services at the time, Russ Seigelman, raised a key question that remained unanswered (Stross, 1996), "How do you make money off this thing?"

In light of these complex motivations, Microsoft management formed strategic alliances to cover all the bases in a variety of possible scenarios that it envisioned for the unfolding of the Internet business model (Cusumano and Selby, 1995). Between 1993 and 1995, Microsoft formed over twenty agreements, which gave Microsoft increased access to both "content" and "distribution." In addition, Microsoft saw potential business opportunity in the creation of tools for Internet application development.

Microsoft's content agreements covered a wide spectrum of information, from high-brow to home shopping. For example, Microsoft hired Michael Kinsley, a famous Washington columnist, to develop *Slate;* negotiated content supply agreements with forty-five companies such as Home Shopping Network and Ziff-Davis; and invested in DreamWorks SKG, an entertainment company founded by three Hollywood luminaries.

At the time, Microsoft thought that its content might be distributed over cable lines or telephone lines. Its arrangement with TCI is an example of how Microsoft gained access to cable distribution. Microsoft also made arrangements for distribution over telephone lines and made several agreements for the building of tools to help developers of interactive TV systems.

As Microsoft's Internet business model has evolved, it has become clear that these initial arrangements hedged the uncertainty fairly well. At the time, interactive TV seemed to be a potentially important channel of distribution. In 1996, the promise of interactive TV appeared to have less immediate potential for a significant payoff. Through its arrangements to distribute content over telephone lines, Microsoft was well positioned to launch its Microsoft Network service.

Microsoft initially thought that its business model for on-line services would entail the packaging and distribution of proprietary content. As it became clear that direct access to the Internet was more important to consumers, Microsoft decided to emphasize building market share for its Internet browser, Internet Explorer. Microsoft envisioned that if it could encourage the widespread use of its Web browser, access to the Internet could potentially be a toll road.

For example, in 1996 Microsoft announced an agreement with America Online, a leading on-line information service provider.

This agreement involved AOL's use of Internet Explorer in exchange for easing AOL's access to the Internet from Microsoft's PC operating systems. This agreement simultaneously helped Microsoft expand its share of the Internet browser market against Netscape's Navigator while helping a company that was competing with its Microsoft Network (Stross, 1996).

In the development tools area, Microsoft also changed its strategy. Initially, Microsoft thought that it needed to build an Internet development tool itself. Ultimately, Microsoft decided to license Java, Sun Microsystem's Internet development tool (Microsoft press release, April 30, 1996).

Cisco Systems

According to a June 1996 summary of Cisco Systems acquisitions and minority equity investments, between 1993 and 1996 Cisco completed more than seventeen acquisitions or minority investments. Cisco's acquisitions were driven by its business strategy of providing complete interoperability for its customers. This means that as customers move to new technologies for communication across computer networks, Cisco wants to be the company that sells the new technology to the customer. In addition, Cisco wants to ensure that the new technology can operate efficiently with all other network communications equipment that the company has already installed.

Over the last three years, Cisco Systems's stock has been very highly valued, making it a useful acquisition currency. Cisco used its stock to acquire companies from whom Cisco customers purchased internetworking products. As we will explore in Chapter Four, Cisco has made so many acquisitions that its ability to acquire and manage companies successfully has become an important source of competitive advantage.

According to Heskett (1996), in September 1996 Cisco announced that it would acquire a startup company, Granite Systems, for $220 million in Cisco stock. Acquiring Granite Systems provided Cisco with a quick way to get access to standards-based multilayer Gigabit Ethernet switching technologies.

Why would anyone pay so much money for that? Gigabit Ethernet switching technologies can move data as fast as one billion bits per second, several times faster than competing technologies. Data traffic over corporate networks has been exploding as more employees use the networks. This growth in traffic has been made even worse by the high bandwidth (big data packages) of many corporate applications. These new applications include the Internet, multimedia, and groupware such as Lotus Notes. As a result of this growth in corporate network traffic, users are being frustrated by painfully slow transmissions. Multilayer switching and Gigabit Ethernet may be able to alleviate this traffic congestion.

Cisco and Granite Systems were two of the founding members of a sixty-company industry-standards body, the Gigabit Ethernet Alliance. This alliance is developing a standard that will fit within Cisco's product architecture. Whereas the market for Gigabit Ethernet is estimated to reach a mere $73 million in 1997, Dataquest expects the industry to grow to $3 billion by the year 2000. By acquiring a startup for $220 million, Cisco got a technology that it is betting will provide it with a big piece of a $3 billion market in three years. More important, Cisco will be able to keep pace with the demands of its customers for more and faster data transmission capacity (Heskett, 1996).

The Microsoft and Cisco Systems examples reflect three principles that technology leaders follow when they partner or acquire to close the capability gap:

If your customers need a technology now, acquire—don't build. In order for Cisco to retain the greatest share of its customers' internetworking business, it is better off paying now for the segment leader. If Cisco waits to develop the technology internally, it risks losing its share of a fast-growing market.

In high-growth markets, acquisition can create a bigger pie for both parties. Cisco learned the power of this principle when it acquired a stake in Cascade Communications. In December 1993, Cisco's stake was valued at $2.75 million. By September 1996, that stake was worth $276 million, a one hundred to one payoff.

If there is substantial uncertainty about how an industry will evolve, bet carefully on more than one scenario. Microsoft bet on two distribution scenarios for its Internet strategy. When one channel developed more slowly than the other, the different development rates did not slow down Microsoft.

CEO Change Agenda

Having reviewed the practices of technology leaders for managing core technologies, what should CEOs do to adopt them?

Form a team to make an inventory of all of the firm's technologies. The team should make an effort to identify the potential products that could be based on these technologies. For each potential product, the team needs to identify and analyze its potential markets. Teams should estimate market size, growth rate, and trends driving profitability. The teams should understand the specific sources of customer value creation and determine whether any competitors have the technology and how difficult the technology may be to replicate.

Rank technologies based on a composite score that integrates the three criteria for judging core technologies. Noncore technologies, at the bottom of the list, should be syndicated, as we will see in Chapter Four.

Value core technologies based on the net present value of the cash flows they would generate if they achieved reasonable market penetration. These cash inflows should be offset by the investments required to develop, manufacture, and distribute the products generated by these technologies.

Analyze technologies from the outside in. Teams should listen to current customers and understand their needs. Teams should identify any gaps between the firm's current technologies and the technologies required to meet customer needs.

Determine the most effective and efficient way to obtain these "gap" technologies. The team should examine many alternatives, including potential acquisitions, strategic partnerships, and internal development. These alternatives should be ranked based on the expected time to market; cost of development, investment, or acquisition; and expected return.

Establish an ongoing mechanism to monitor technologies that could undermine the firm's basic operating model. Make managers accountable for taking advantage of the opportunities presented by changing technologies.

Chapter Four examines how to identify and manage noncore technologies and explores how technology leaders "rent" noncore technologies. It highlights some of the most significant challenges to managing these technology alliances and provides examples of how technology leaders meet these challenges.

Open Technology II
Syndicating the Noncore

Technology leaders recognize that although noncore technologies are not strategic, they consume resources that could be invested in core technologies and other capabilities that create value for customers. Technology leaders therefore pursue a systematic approach to syndicating noncore technologies, a practice that frees up resources for investment in more strategic areas.

Noncore technologies fall into two categories. *Outplaced* technologies are formerly core technologies whose value to customers, competitive uniqueness, or applicability to a wide variety of markets has faded. *Outsourced* technologies are those that the firm needs to "rent" from a third party for a specific project but that the firm does not want to add to its base of fixed costs.

The concept of syndicating noncore technologies suggests an underlying mindset that is similar to that used by arbitrageurs. Arbitrage is the process of buying a commodity in one market where it is inexpensive and selling the commodity in another market where it is more expensive. Arbitrageurs understand that these price differences between markets are temporary. In order to exploit price differences, however, they must do more than simply trade. They must gain access to capabilities, such as processing and distribution, that enable them to get their commodity to the higher-paying market.

This creates a dilemma. Arbitrageurs must gain access to these nontrading capabilities, but if they invest in these capabilities, they risk being stuck with illiquid assets long after the arbitrage opportunity has ceased to exist.

The story of a financial firm, Louis Dreyfus & Cie, described in *Forbes* (Levine, 1996), provides some insight into these matters. Louis Dreyfus, founded in 1850 in France, trades around $22 billion per year in commodities, including wheat, cotton, treasury bills, petroleum products, and natural gas. Under the parent company, it owns over two million square feet of office space in North America and Europe. It owns twenty-one cargo vessels. It is the third largest processor of orange juice. It makes particleboard in Brazil and Argentina. And it owns the license for Ralph Lauren clothing in Europe.

Louis Dreyfus's "core technology" is arbitrage. The specific commodities that the firm has traded since its founding in 1850, and the capabilities that it has developed to arbitrage these commodities, are the firm's "noncore technologies." The first postwar generation had thought of the family firm as a grain trader, whereas William, the founder's great-grandson, realized that it was in the arbitrage business. William Louis-Dreyfus drew the analogy between a microbe and an arbitrageur. Dreyfus pointed out that a microbe inhabits a person's body, enjoys its stay, but ultimately kills its host (and itself in the bargain). Similarly, when an arbitrageur sees a market inefficiency, he goes to it and makes it efficient, eliminating his profit in the process (Levine, 1996).

Louis Dreyfus's core technology, arbitrage, has survived. Its noncore technologies—trading in grain, oil, and gas—have fluctuated in their value to the company.

In 1850, Leopold Dreyfus began carting wheat from his family's farm at Sierentz, in France's Alsace region, to Basel, Switzerland. Leopold, at seventeen too young to name the firm after himself, named it after his father, Louis. He soon began trading to other local farms and in 1851 incorporated the first international grain-trading business. Within ten years he was trading grain throughout the continent, buying and selling wherever he could detect a worthwhile spread between prices.

Leopold recognized that long-term success depended on his ability to limit risks so that no individual trade could bankrupt his firm. When the Liverpool Corn Trade Association authorized futures trading in 1883, Leopold was one of the first grain merchants to buy and sell simultaneously, thereby locking in a spread. For example, he purchased grain from Russian peasants around the Black Sea and then telegraphed his British agents to sell the same quantity for local delivery at a specified price that included transportation, storage, insurance, and a guaranteed profit. By the time Leopold died in 1915, Louis Dreyfus & Cie was the largest international grain merchant.

Although the company survived World War I, the founder's grandsons Jean, Francois, and Pierre scattered when Germany invaded Paris in World War II. After the war, Jean and Francois tried to rebuild the grain business, while Pierre developed Louis Dreyfus's cargo vessel fleet. Wheat, however, had become less profitable, using scarce capital to secure slender profit margins. At the same time, Cargill and Continental Grain bought flour mills and other processing businesses to enhance trading margins. Louis Dreyfus ignored processing, dropping from first to fifth in the industry among the major industry participants.

As the firm's position dropped, another family member, William Louis-Dreyfus, joined the company in 1965. By 1969, at age thirty-seven, he was the chief executive. In 1972, he hired seven traders from Memphis-based Cook Industries, a grain and cotton merchant. The Cook traders changed Louis Dreyfus & Cie into a company that could arbitrage many commodity markets, including government bonds, rice, cotton, meat, and oil. By 1990, its trading volume had increased fivefold over its 1972 level.

In 1985, Daniel Finn, one of the Cook traders, saw an opportunity in the oil business that at the time suffered from excess supply and volatile prices. Whereas the major oil companies built up oil stocks or depleted them depending on where they forecast oil prices to be, Louis Dreyfus bought oil on the spot market and simultaneously sold it directly to end users for future delivery. The firm compared the price at which it could purchase oil on the current day, the cost of storing oil out into the future, and the price at which it could be sold for future delivery. For a year, Louis Dreyfus was able to earn attractive returns. This opportunity ended as the arbitrage evened out excessive fluctuations in the oil market, thereby destroying its own profitability.

At this point, Louis Dreyfus chose not to repeat the same mistake in petroleum that it had made in grain. The company used its crude oil arbitrage profits to lease a network of oil storage terminals from Tenneco and then bought a storage network from Unocal in 1992. By 1996, the company was moving seventy-three million barrels of refined petroleum products through its network of thirty-two terminals and 350 delivery points. The terminals enabled Louis Dreyfus to manage the basis risk in refined petroleum, putting itself in a position to negotiate long-term contracts for heating oil, gas, and diesel fuel.

How does the Louis Dreyfus example relate to syndicating noncore technologies? Although noncore technologies are not often thought of as commodities that are traded in large, well-established markets, there are important analogies.

Louis Dreyfus recognizes that its core "technology" is arbitrage. Its noncore "technologies" are trading in wheat, oil, gas, and electricity. Technology leaders recognize that their core technology may be a broad source of customer value creation that extends beyond any specific technology. For example, Cisco's core technology is providing a seamless integration of its customers' internetworking technologies; its noncore technologies are the various devices, such as hubs, routers, and switches, that facilitate this interconnection. When firms confuse noncore and core technologies, they initiate a sequence of decisions that can have potentially expensive consequences.

Louis Dreyfus recognized, with varying degrees of speed over its history, that specific arbitrage opportunities, or noncore technologies, vary in value and are in fact self-defeating over time. Technology leaders recognize that the value of their noncore technologies will build and then erode. Technology leaders recognize this cycle, driven by the tendency of many industries to become "perfectly competitive" over time, and take appropriate action. For example, they use the cash generated by noncore technologies at the peak in the cycle to invest in new technologies with high economic potential. And once a noncore technology has lost its ability to produce high economic value, it is shed—licensed or sold to the highest bidder.

Louis Dreyfus was unafraid of entering new businesses in which it did not appear to have sufficient expertise. Technology leaders branch out into new businesses where their core technologies will give them a competitive advantage. Firms like Louis Dreyfus, and technology leaders, believe in their ability to find partners, either through joint ventures or acquisitions, who can lend their industry-specific expertise to the fundamental advantages that the technology leaders bring through their core technologies.

The remainder of this chapter explores how technology leaders identify noncore technologies, syndicate noncore technologies, and manage external partnerships.

Identifying Noncore Technologies

Before a firm can manage its noncore technologies, it must first identify them. Chapter Three described techniques that technology leaders use to identify their core technologies. Many technologies do not satisfy the criteria required to make them part of the core. These technologies are called *outplaced* technologies, because technology leaders apply various approaches to place them outside the firm's operations. These technologies no longer create sufficient customer value or economic value to the firm to justify their consumption of capital resources.

In parallel with the process of identifying these outplaced technologies, technology leaders identify *outsourced* technologies that are required for specific projects but that the firm does not want to add to its base of fixed costs.

When technology leaders decide to go after specific market segments, they seek insights into the specific capabilities required for competitive success. To the extent that they possess all the essential capabilities internally, they may not need to look outside to compete in these new markets. On the other hand, if there are important capabilities that they do not possess but that are required in order to compete effectively, they may seek to outsource them. Specific process steps include the following:

Generate new market ideas, based on listening to current customers or on analyzing industry trends. For example, Cisco generates many ideas for adding to its technology portfolio by monitoring the technology spending patterns of its customers. Microsoft analyzed the growing popularity of the Internet and recognized that it needed to build its capabilities in this area in order to maintain its share of the desktop.

Screen these potential markets based on size, growth rate, and profitability. As several venture capitalists have pointed out, if you are looking to invest the same amount in two new ventures, it is better to put money into the one that is going after the larger market. When Cisco Systems spent $220 million on Granite Systems, it was betting that it would get a good chunk of a market that was growing from virtually nothing to $3 billion in three years.

Analyze unmet customer needs in these segments and study the technologies and capabilities required to meet these needs. When J&J talked to the customers of its Ethicon division, it found out that they needed stents. So J&J licensed the stent from two scientists and grew it into a significant business.

Assess the firm's capabilities relative to segment requirements. Before Merck decided to buy Medco, it was missing a critical capability. In a fairly short period of time, pricing power had shifted from the pharmaceutical companies to the payers. Merck alone was quite capable of raising its prices every year to increase revenues. What Merck could not do quite as easily on its own was to increase revenues in an environment where drug prices would be dropping. Merck perceived that Medco would help Merck make up for dropping prices through increased volume.

Syndicating Noncore Technologies: Outplacing

Technology leaders have made noncore technology deals so frequently that the ability to make these deals has become a source of competitive advantage. The advantage comes from being able to negotiate terms that give the technology leader access to the technology that it needs without incurring too much cost.

Amgen

Since 1984, Amgen, America's most profitable biotechnology company, has implemented more than thirty-seven strategic alliances. These alliances involved cash payments of over $600 million, equity investments in excess of $80 million, and royalties ranging from 10 percent to 60 percent of revenues.

Amgen is very clever in the way it negotiates these deals. In exchange for the right to market a technology that it has developed in its labs, Amgen gets cash payments from its "deep pocketed" partner. These cash payments are received not only when the deal is signed but also at key development and marketing milestones.

Amgen is thus able to develop, promote, and market a noncore technology without consuming scarce capital. Amgen's partner gets a valuable technology that can potentially be developed into a product that covers its manufacturing and marketing costs.

In June 1996, Amgen and Yamanouchi Pharmaceuticals, a Tokyo-based pharmaceutical company, announced that Amgen had licensed to Yamanouchi the rights to develop, manufacture, and commercialize Amgen's Consensus Interferon (CIFN) in all countries except the United States and Canada. (In these two countries, Amgen planned to market CIFN as Infergen.) The license was the result of a five-month process involving twelve pharmaceutical companies that had expressed an interest in CIFN.

Market: CIFN is a treatment for Hepatitis C virus (HCV) infection, a common cause of chronic hepatitis, cirrhosis, and a form of liver cancer. In a North American clinical trial, CIFN was shown to be more effective than a competing product, interferon alfa 2b, for patients infected with HCV genotype 1. This genotype accounts for 60 percent of North American HCV patients and 70 to 80 percent of Japanese HCV patients.

Terms: Yamanouchi paid $15 million on signing the license. Yamanouchi agreed to additional payments several times that amount depending on meeting certain milestones. Yamanouchi also contracted to pay royalties on sales and granted Amgen's Japanese and Chinese subsidiaries specific codevelopment, copromotion, and comarketing rights.

Benefits to Amgen: Amgen benefited from Yamanouchi's signing payment. Amgen also obtained assurances of additional investment for development and marketing of the technology. In addition, Amgen benefits from the incremental Asian revenues that Yamanouchi's marketing channels will generate.

Benefits to Yamanouchi: Yamanouchi valued Amgen's technology, which it perceived to be the basis for an important product to add to its global distribution network ("Amgen Announcement of Yamanouchi Agreement," 1996).

In negotiating this deal, Amgen followed principles that guide technology leaders in managing noncore technologies. Amgen analyzed the potential geographic markets for the compound and decided to keep for itself the marketing rights for the most profitable segments. Amgen identified the development, manufacturing, and distribution capabilities that it needed to get from a partner in order to maximize the product's potential value. Amgen then negotiated with many potential partners who could possibly provide these capabilities, ultimately selecting the partner that offered the best mix of cash and capabilities. Finally, the terms of the transaction enabled Amgen to recoup some of its investment in the development of the compound. The deal created incentives to achieve specific development milestones and gave Amgen a share of the revenues that its partner might generate.

Frequently, competitors execute cross-licensing agreements to settle patent litigation. The parties benefit by terminating the costs of litigation. They also gain by sharing technologies that can be used to increase the overall market, creating greater revenues for both parties. These agreements combine outplacing and outsourcing noncore technologies.

In the Bay Networks–3Com agreement, the two companies settled patent litigation by agreeing to work together to increase the overall market. The Intel-AMD agreement settled patent litigation through undisclosed payments from AMD and through an agreement that increased the size of the pie for both parties.

Bay Networks–3Com

These two vendors of networking hardware and software announced in November 1995 that they had signed a cooperative mutual patent license agreement. This agreement covered all patents held by both companies and extended to all patents issued to both organizations for five years. According to the agreement, cross-royalty payments, based on publicly reported research and development expenses, could not exceed $12 million by either company.

In conjunction with the agreement, both parties fully resolved and settled patent litigation that both sides had initiated. According to 3Com's CEO, the agreement created an R&D environment that would shorten time to market for differentiated products, accelerating the growth of the networking industry. Bay Network's CEO commented that the agreement would enable his engineers to implement the best design features without constraint ("Patents: Bay Networks and 3Com . . .," 1995).

AMD–Intel

These two semiconductor vendors announced in January 1996 that they had agreed on a five-year patent cross-licensing agreement that completed the settlement of a long-standing legal dispute between the two companies. The agreement enabled AMD to continue designing and marketing x86-compatible processors without legal attacks from Intel. Furthermore, although it did not access microcode copyrights, AMD did obtain the copyrights and patents it needed to implement Intel's multimedia extensions (MMX) in its future processors.

Intel gained access to AMD's patent portfolio and received undisclosed royalty payments from AMD. More broadly, Intel benefited from the agreement by helping establish MMX as an industry standard. Intel and AMD were also able to increase the x86 market. Intel was able to use its fabrication capacity more fully while gaining a six- to twelve-month lead over non-AMD competitors such as Cyrix ("AMD Gains Access . . .," 1996).

Syndicating Noncore Technologies: Outsourcing

The converse of outplacing noncore technologies that have outlived their value to the firm is outsourcing them. Technology leaders make deals that give them access to alliance technologies—noncore technologies that are required for specific projects.

Technology leaders benefit from these outsourcing deals in several ways. First, they are able to rent a technology that they will need for only a finite amount of time. Second, they have greater flexibility either to increase their ownership stake in the technology or eliminate their involvement altogether. Finally, by working with other organizations, technology leaders may learn about a new technology or a new business process that could be valuable to its customers.

Amgen negotiates deals that give it access to potentially useful technologies without incurring the full cost of ownership. These deals include an up-front cash payment as well as payments linked to specific development milestones. In addition, Amgen acquires minority stakes in the companies, enabling Amgen to influence its partner's strategic direction and to take advantage of potential upside returns without buying the whole company. Finally, these deals often enable Amgen to broaden its product portfolio in a segment of the market in which it had already built a strong position.

In December 1995, Amgen and NPS Pharmaceuticals, a Salt Lake City–based development stage company founded in 1986, signed a letter of intent to collaborate in the development and commercialization of NPS's Norcalcin, a treatment for hyperparathyroidism (HPT), a disease resulting from kidney failure that affects up to 80 percent of dialysis patients.

Market: HPT, or excessive parathyroid secretions, produces elevated serum calcium. Symptoms may include bone loss, hypertension, gastrointestinal distress, muscle weakness, depression, and forgetfulness. In the United States, there are roughly 250,000 cases of the disease, about two-thirds of which are women.

Terms: Amgen paid NPS an initial license fee of $10 million, with potential additional milestone payments totaling $26 million, plus royalties on product sales. Amgen also agreed to purchase one million shares of NPS stock for $7.5 million, a price set to equal NPS's stock price in November 1995, when the stock purchase negotiations were initiated. Amgen received exclusive worldwide rights (excluding Japan, China, Korea, and Taiwan) to develop and sell Norcalcin, which was in Phase I/II clinical trials at the time of the announcement. Both parties participated in development, but Amgen paid all costs of developing and commercializing products.

Benefits to Amgen: Amgen benefited in two ways: by gaining access to a potential treatment for a currently unmet medical need and by strengthening Amgen's position in the U.S. market for the treatment of kidney diseases. Amgen had previously discovered and developed Epogen to treat anemia experienced by patients on dialysis who experience chronic renal failure. Amgen also gained access to a new group of patients outside the United States.

Benefits to NPS: NPS valued Amgen's strong presence in the renal field and its interest in endocrinology. NPS also gained access to Amgen's prior work with the pharmaceutical division of Kirin Brewery—NPS's corporate partner for Norcalcin in Asia. NPS received $25 million in cash after closing the Amgen agreement, coupled with potential milestone payments of $39 million plus royalties from Amgen and Kirin. These and other payments helped NPS reduce its "cash burn" and accelerate its product development capabilities ("Amgen Announcement of NPS Alliance," 1996).

✕✕✕

The Amgen example demonstrates several of the principles that technology leaders follow in structuring outsourcing deals.

Analyze the profit potential of the market in which the technology would be sold. In following this principle, Amgen saw that it could increase its profits from the renal market by broadening its product portfolio with this new technology. Because pharmaceutical customers find it less costly to purchase all their disease-specific treatments from one supplier, Amgen saw a "product portfolio" benefit that would increase its share of the renal market.

Compare the cost and time of developing the technology internally to outsourcing it. Amgen decided it would be cheaper and faster to outsource the gap-filling technology.

Structure the terms of the agreement to limit the licensor's costs, maximize its flexibility, and motivate its partner to commercialize the product as quickly as possible. By structuring the NPS agreement with a finite cash payment up front and incremental payments tied to achieving specific development objectives, Amgen was able to gain the benefits of access to these products without adding much to its fixed costs.

Managing External Partnerships

Negotiating outsourcing deals requires much less management time than does making them work. Indeed, external partnerships present many management challenges, including vague goals and objectives, unclear measures of success, failure to anticipate conflicts, lack of accountability, misgauging distribution requirements, and overestimating demand.

External partnerships can be killed by differences in culture, levels of commitment, and strategic and financial objectives. Such changes in industry structure as regulatory shifts, new technologies, unanticipated new entrants, and slower than expected market growth can also threaten these alliances.

The most successful partnerships occur when both parties have a strong mutual dependence. For example, an effective business relationship can result when a small technology company that needs capital, manufacturing, and distribution forms an alliance with a large company that needs the small company's technology to complete its product portfolio.

If two companies are not mutually dependent, the smaller company gets frustrated by the large company's lack of interest. Conversely, when two large companies form an alliance, it is often difficult to determine which party is dominant, which means that both parties may consume substantial time posturing for position. The joint ventures between GTE and Disney or U.S. West and Time Warner exemplify these difficulties.

Often partnerships are announced with great fanfare, primarily to create the perception that management is taking action to participate in a market that is currently fashionable. If both parties do not commit respected executives and valuable resources to these partnerships, it is likely that their strategic intent may be too muted to result in a successful partnership. Industry consortia are often less than effective in achieving their objectives. For example, an information technology consortium that had been established to agree on a standard for interoperability did not achieve its objective; it ultimately endorsed TCP/IP after the majority of customers decided to adopt it as the standard.

In order to manage these partnerships effectively and avoid many of the pitfalls just described, technology leaders take the following steps:

1. *Share objectives.* In order for a partnership to be successful, participants must share common objectives. For example, Intel and Microsoft's partnership has created big benefits for both sides. Microsoft gets cheap processing power, and Intel gets software that converts this power into PCs that large numbers of people will pay for. Without shared objectives, subsequent steps are irrelevant.

2. *Assign respected executives from both firms to be accountable for the success of the venture.* Many ventures fail because the accountability for their success is vague or the individuals responsible for their success lack the level of respect and authority within each organization to direct the resources required to ensure their success. By assigning clear accountability, preferably to individuals who were actively involved in negotiating the alliance agreement, both parties signal that they have an interest in its success.

3. *Create internal teams.* Having been assigned to manage the partnership, accountable executives must build the teams from various parts of their organizations that will actually do the work. In selecting people for the project, it is important to identify individuals who will be able to contribute functional expertise and also work effectively with individuals outside their own organizations and outside the company. Once the individuals have been selected, it is often useful to sponsor team-building exercises that enable all participants to become comfortable with each other at a personal and professional level. These team-building meetings should also transfer any content knowledge or analytical tools that may enhance the team's productivity.

4. *Develop a business plan for the venture.* After assigning accountable executives and creating the teams that will do the work, all must agree on what they jointly intend to accomplish. The teams should develop a business plan that includes measurable objectives and a set of strategic initiatives to achieve these objectives. The plan should also make clear what information is appropriate to share and, perhaps more important, what information is off-limits.

5. *Link incentives to project objectives.* All participants should have a clear understanding of how their personal performance objectives are linked to the project objectives. At predetermined stages in the project, the performance of the accountable project executives and their teams should be assessed relative to these objectives. A bonus pool that constitutes a substantial portion of compensation should be awarded based on the extent to which the objectives are achieved. Furthermore, future career assignments should be linked to performance relative to project objectives. In many companies, project participants are perceived as not doing "real" work that benefits their bosses, and as a result they lose opportunities for financial compensation and promotions.

6. *Create mechanisms for conflict resolution.* Tension often exists within partnerships because a partner in one market may be a competitor in another market. Tensions also arise simply because of cultural differences between the two firms that were not considered "deal killers" during negotiations. Technology leaders create organizational mechanisms for handling such conflicts. For example, they may require accountable executives to identify and monitor information that is passed between participants. If conflicts among partners cannot be resolved at lower levels, there may be formal or informal mechanisms for resolving them at the CEO, chairman, or board of directors levels, if necessary. Ultimately, if conflicts cannot be resolved, they may initiate the termination of the partnership.

7. *Develop a clear vision for ending the partnership.* An important element of the partnership's business plan is a clear vision of the conditions under which the partnership will end. If these conditions are vague, the partnership risks consuming capital and management time without having a clear end in mind. Furthermore, setting clear conditions for terminating the partnership tends to focus participants on achieving its objectives efficiently.

Cisco Systems has developed an approach to managing its acquisitions that provides useful guidance for managing the business partnerships discussed in this chapter. John Chambers, Cisco's CEO, managed six successful acquisitions between January 1995 (when he became CEO) and June 1996. Chambers believed that 50 percent of acquisitions fail because they overlook "the basics." In his view successful acquisitions must pass five tests (Nee, 1996):

1. *Do both parties share a common vision of the future of the industry?* For example, at the time that Cisco made its equity investment in Cascade, both companies perceived that the market was consolidating and that customers chose vendors based on how well they integrated products. When Cisco acquired StrataCom, both companies shared a view that growth opportunities would come from the ability to eliminate the bottlenecks that have slowed Internet transmission speeds. Cisco perceived that its customers would benefit from Cisco's routing skills and StrataCom's strengths in very high-end WAN switches for data, ATM, and frame-relay.

2. *Do the product strategies of both parties complement each other or compete?* When Cisco made its investment in Cascade their product lines did not overlap. Over time, however, Cascade began to enter Cisco's product area, particularly in the dial-up market, and began to align itself with IBM. The Cascade alliance thus began to fail this second test. Cisco needed to decide whether to move closer to Cascade, possibly by acquiring the company, or to compete with Cascade. Cisco's decision to acquire StrataCom reflects its decision to compete with Cascade by purchasing what Cisco perceived to be the leading firm in the industry segment.

3. *Can the combination create "short-term wins"?* For example, there was a 14 percent average drop in the stock the week following the announcement of three networking industry transactions: Wellfleet-SynOptics, 3Com-Chipcom, and Fore-Alantec. On the other hand, the week after Cisco announced its acquisition of StrataCom, Cisco's stock rose 10 percent. Chambers suggested that Cisco's stock rose because equity holders understood the financial benefits that the deal would create.

4. *Does the combination create "long-term wins" for all strategic constituents?* For example, in December 1993 Cisco made a $2.9 million equity investment in Cascade, a provider of frame-relay switches, creating a profit of over $200 million by June 1996.

5. *Are the cultures of both parties alike, and are they complementary?* When Cisco acquired StrataCom, the fact that the two companies were geographically close enhanced management credibility: executives could look employees in the eye and tell them that they would not lay off employees. As it turned out, Cisco had six hundred open positions and StrataCom had one hundred openings. Both their cultural similarities and the complementary nature of their technologies contributed to this growth.

As Chambers points out, partnerships that do not satisfy all of these criteria tend to fail. He suggests that IBM's acquisition of Rolm, a vendor of PBXs, in the 1980s failed three out of five of these tests. The two companies had very different visions of the direction of the industry, their cultures were very different and separated geographically, and the long-term "win-win" was missing for both participants (Nee, 1996). Ultimately, as is true for all the practices outlined in this chapter, the critical element is discipline: if all five of the tests are not met, a partnership should not proceed.

Chapter Five shows how technology leaders link their people and technology to create products that customers value. It highlights the specific advantages that flow to companies that choose boundaryless product development. The advantages of this process are illustrated through specific examples from technology leaders.

Boundaryless Product Development I
Running Fast Teams

Technology leaders manage their people and technology to create products that customers eagerly buy. They do this by choosing a boundaryless approach to product development, which opens communication channels that would otherwise be clogged. In peer companies, there are boundaries between functions within the firm, and even higher barriers between the companies and their suppliers and customers.

Technology leaders make better products because they mix the ideas of different participants. They identify problems early, before too much money has been spent. By looking at design problems from different perspectives they get ideas that would not have emerged from any individual function working by itself. And, because they don't leave out important participants, they are not blindsided at the last minute.

Peer companies, on the other hand, seem to follow the *Field of Dreams* approach—if you build it, (the customers) will come. Two technologies that suffered from this approach are artificial intelligence and CD-I.

Artificial intelligence. In the early 1980s a former computer science professor raised over $15 million in venture capital from an insurance company. The objective was to cash in on an exciting new technology: artificial intelligence. More specifically, the ex-professor wanted to build an expert system for personal financial planning.

An expert system is a software program that captures the rules of thumb that experts use to make professional decisions. The idea was that if you could capture the accumulated wisdom of the leading experts in a particular field of study, you could spread that expertise to more customers. For example, an expert system for personal financial planning might record such details as how a planner goes about deciding the right mix of stocks, bonds, and cash for a particular client.

Knowledge engineers and programmers were hired to begin work on the product. The knowledge engineers met with experts in personal financial planning and interviewed them to map out their decision rules. The programmers wrote software that encoded these rules.

Eventually, the company developed a prototype of the program. They decided to approach personal financial planners (mostly insurance agents) to sell them the product. The personal financial planners did not share the enthusiasm of the expert systems developers. They found the system too complex, too difficult to use, and too expensive. So the expert systems company went back to the drawing boards and developed a smaller, less complex version. By this time, the company employed eighty people.

What happened? The company kept trying to sell its prototype and eventually burned through the venture capital without generating significant revenue. Beneath the surface of personal financial planners' comments on the early version of the product was a fear that the system would cost them their jobs. Or it may have been that the technology simply did not create enough customer value to justify the price of the product and the cost to set it up and learn how to use it.

CD-I. In fall 1991, Philips Electronics NV introduced CD-I. This compact disc–interactive player was thought of as so versatile that it was called "the Imagination Machine." The product was a game player, a teaching tool, and a music game. Philips management believed that this machine would take the U.S. market by storm, setting a new standard that would give consumers all the high-tech gadgetry they wanted.

What happened? After five years and an estimated $1 billion in development costs, the product has generally disappeared from consumer retail shelves. Although Philips continues to market its system to educational and professional markets, it has quietly conceded that the product will not be the consumer success it had once envisioned.

Why? At the core, Philips was trying to push a technology into a market that it did not understand. Philips angered its development partners; product features changed; and the product price was too high. And its distribution and advertising tactics were less than effective.

The CD-I product had its origin in a successful joint venture between Philips and Sony. Philips was respected for its engineering skills, Sony for its consumer electronics marketing ability. The partners launched a successful audio cassette and succeeded again with the compact disc player. In creating CD-I, they hoped to repeat their success with a venture to extend the compact disc format. Matsushita Electric Industries, a leading consumer electronics maker, also agreed to support CD-I.

Philips and Sony needed to agree on hundreds of design specifications for the system that required specialized semiconductors. Software developers hoping to make titles for the new system got frustrated by the inevitable delays. In addition, Philips was reluctant to disclose complex technological specifications to Sony and Matsushita. As a result, Philips had to launch the product in the United States without the marketing clout that its Japanese partners would have provided.

Philips's inexperience in marketing contributed to its indecision about product features and pricing. Initially, the system was promoted as an interactive teaching aid for children and their parents, then as a digital-photo gadget, and finally as a machine for kids who like computer games. By the time Philips latched onto the video game idea, in 1994, it was too late. Although a technical and critical success, its science fiction game *Burn: Cycle* never became the breakthrough title that Philips needed to drive its sales.

Philips also insisted on selling the players for $799 even though marketing people told the company to introduce CD-I at $399. By June 1994, the system, complete with the video cartridge, was still priced above $500, more than twice the price of competing systems from Sega and Nintendo. Philips was determined to recoup its investment in the technology by using a high price.

Philips wanted early adopters to help introduce the product into the U.S. market. One such company, a seven-store consumer electronics chain in Southern California, was stunned when it saw that it took consumers thirty minutes to learn how to use the product. When Philips tried to sell the product to larger stores, one hundred trainers were dispatched to explain how the product worked. Philips also installed over one thousand in-store demonstration kiosks at a cost of $900 each to encourage shoppers to explore the product on their own.

Despite the additional training, clerks made more money selling TVs and VCRs. It took over thirty minutes to sell the system, and people were stealing them from the kiosks. With sales falling behind plan, Philips commissioned a thirty-minute infomercial in fall 1993. Unlike most infomercials, which solicit orders directly, this one directed viewers to the nearest retailer via an 800 number. Philips lost thousands of impulse sales (Trachtenberg, 1996).

The artificial intelligence and CD-I examples illustrate some of the pitfalls of this *Field of Dreams* approach to product development. In both cases, the proponents of the new product took great pride in their engineering prowess. They believed that when customers had the chance to see the brilliance of the companies' designs, they would eagerly purchase their products. When the expected result did not materialize, both companies stumbled in search of a solution. In neither case did they attend to what their customers really wanted to buy. They assumed that a simple tweaking of product features and pricing would solve the problem. Finally, they ran out of money.

Technology leaders don't have these problems. They replace the intellectual arrogance demonstrated in these two cases with intellectual humility. Technology leaders open their minds to changes in customer needs, technologies, and competitive behavior. This difference in executive outlook generates profound differences in the product development process. These practices are briefly discussed here; following this introduction, each will be elaborated upon with examples.

Building cross-functional teams. Technology leaders have learned how to use cross-functional teams effectively. On particularly complex projects, these teams consist of a moderate number of subteams that specialize in specific aspects of the overall problem. In order to make these teams work, technology leaders create effective mechanisms for reintegrating the work of these subteams.

These teams include division managers and managers from such functions as purchasing, finance, human resources, research, manufacturing, marketing, and sales. Team participants are selected based on their ability to think creatively; their capacity to work well with other team participants; their knowledge and experience in the specific industries to be analyzed; and their ability to make decisions despite substantial uncertainty. These teams may often be supplemented with external consultants who can help structure and facilitate the process, offer independent research capabilities, and analyze information objectively.

Peer companies, although many are familiar with the concept of cross-functional teams, have not succeeded in implementing them.

Deploying project plans. Technology leaders use project planning frameworks that evolve over time to reflect organizational learning. Although these frameworks differ by industry and product, they serve the important purpose of allowing management to assess the expected value of competing projects. These project plans also force subteams to link project components. Technology leaders thus avoid the problem of having parts that work better individually than together as a system.

Involving early adopters. Technology leaders work closely with early adopters as they develop new products. Because the mass market relies on early adopters to develop a standard product, early adopters help determine who wins the battle for market leadership. Technology leaders listen to early adopters as they describe their unmet needs. Furthermore, technology leaders observe the way that early adopters use existing products, to gain greater insight into those product features with the greatest potential for improvement.

Peer companies often assume that they already understand customer needs; they therefore may not perform market research at all, or they perform market research after the product has been designed and manufactured.

Using prototypes. Technology leaders develop prototypes early in the development process. These prototypes unify the work of the cross-functional team and provide customers with something to which they can react. Technology leaders modify these prototypes as they are tested by team participants. By the time the product is ready for customer shipment, it is free of operating defects, is relatively simple and inexpensive to manufacture, and meets real customer needs.

Peer companies, on the other hand, may not develop a prototype until the R&D department has completed its design. This prototype is used to help "sell" the product to a business unit. If the business unit is interested, the prototype may be handed to manufacturing, who in all likelihood will then request a thorough redesign to make it more efficient to manufacture.

Bridging the gap between early adopters and the mass market. Technology leaders recognize that in order to generate substantial revenues from their new products, they will need to convince the mass market to buy them. After satisfying early adopters, technology leaders customize their product to meet the needs of an underserved segment of the market that has a compelling reason to buy. If technology leaders can dominate such segments, their product may then be perceived as an industry standard. If they achieve this perception, technology leaders then develop "product supply engines" to meet growth in demand while maintaining quality and delivery-time requirements.

The remainder of this chapter explores each of these product development phases, illustrating them with examples from technology leaders and peer companies. It concludes with a CEO change agenda that executives can use to help close the gap between their company and technology leaders.

Building Cross-Functional Teams

Much has been written about the virtues of cross-functional teams. They are touted as a means of shortening time to market, lowering cost, and increasing market acceptance for new products.

Many technology leaders have grappled successfully with the organizational challenges that are associated with making the transformation from a relay race approach to a cross-functional team approach. Hewlett-Packard and Schlumberger have successfully executed this transformation.

Hewlett-Packard

Before HP achieved its success in the laser printer and inkjet printer markets, the company placed engineers at the top of its functional hierarchy. HP developed many of its products using what it called the "next bench" approach (Dean Morton, personal communication, May 10, 1996). HP moved into the laser printer market knowing that Canon was the best vendor in the world for supplying laser printing technology. HP's CEO brought a team to Japan to observe Canon's operations and realized that in order for HP to succeed in this market, it would need to change its approach to product development. In particular, HP chose to elevate the role of manufacturing and marketing to a level equal to engineering. This new approach to product development was attempted at its Vancouver facility; it was so successful that it became a model for other HP divisions.

Schlumberger

Schlumberger, a leader in the oil services business, executed a similar transformation of its product development process.

Seventy years ago, Schlumberger invented a business called "wireline logging," a process by which a ten-foot-long metal pole containing an electrical monitoring system was used to pinpoint the location of oil, gas, or water in a hole drilled for oil exploration. Schlumberger carried this pole on a truck with a spool of wire connected to a data recording and analysis instrument. When a hole had been drilled, the pole was lowered to the bottom and then pulled up at ten-foot intervals. Every ten feet, an electrical current was injected into the pole, and a sensor on the pole recorded the electrical response of the surrounding geology. This response was fed back to the data recorder, and, depending on the results of various tests, the Schlumberger field engineer could determine the depth at which the hydrocarbons were located.

Like HP, Schlumberger had a long tradition of engineering being the dominant function. In response to client demands for greater efficiency in their oil exploration processes, Schlumberger management decided to create a fundamental cultural change. This decision led to a new product development process that reduced cycle times by 50 percent. The most important element of this new process was the creation of product development teams. These teams consist of engineering and manufacturing specialists who share common managers and occupy new physical facilities designed specifically to accommodate these teams (from an interview with Victor Grijalva, executive vice president of Schlumberger, May 22, 1996).

The relay race approach to product development, which both of these companies formerly used, is well established and continues today in many companies. In this process, R&D develops an innovation and tries to sell a business unit on turning the design into a revenue-generating product. If R&D succeeds in getting the business unit's attention, R&D may then supply the blueprints and an engineering model to the business unit manager. The business unit may then supply these items to the sales and manufacturing departments. Frequently, the sales force responds that the innovation is not what customers want or that it is two years too late (or too early) to generate significant revenues. Manufacturing may suggest that the innovation costs too much to make, that it requires retooling the manufacturing line or purchasing supplies that are not available from an established supplier. After receiving this feedback, R&D may decide that the innovation is not worth pursuing, or it may take the feedback and redo its design. Although this relay race approach persists in many companies today, it slows time to market, raises development and product costs, and lowers market penetration as compared with the cross-functional team approach.

The cross-functional team approach strives to integrate functions. Although the specific composition of these teams varies by industry and by company, it is typical for these teams to include specialists in disciplines such as engineering, manufacturing, finance, purchasing, logistics, marketing, customer service, and sales. Although these teams may be perceived as difficult to coordinate, they create fundamental benefits that far outweigh the cost of coordinating them:

Communication across functions lowers costs. For example, in the relay race approach, if a design that R&D developed is too expensive to manufacture, a mutual blaming process consumes valuable time and resources. Cross-functional teams work more smoothly to achieve the shared objective of creating a product that offers competitively superior customer value.

Communication across functions reduces time. At Schlumberger, for example, handoffs between engineering and manufacturing have been reduced, leading to shorter product development cycles.

Technology leaders create financial and psychological incentives that reinforce cross-functional teams and instill a sense of pride in what team participants are doing. Teams get a deeper understanding of how the skills of the entire organization can be coordinated to create superior value for customers.

As the Hewlett-Packard and Schlumberger examples illustrate, there are several common elements to a successful transformation from the relay race approach to the cross-functional team approach to product development:

Executive leadership. Any cultural change requires CEO leadership. For change to be effective, the CEO must become actively involved in developing the rationale for the change. The CEO must also choose an outside organization that can serve as a model of effective product development.

Internal prototype. Fundamental change cannot be forced onto an organization. CEO leadership is essential, but the leadership must create an example of how the organization will work under the new process. This example can be studied by the rest of the organization, and the effective processes can then be adopted in a way that is more organic and hence more likely to be viable over the long term.

Alignment. Organizations are finely attuned to whether senior management views something as a short-term fad or a fundamen-

tal cultural change. A key signal to the organization is who partic-
ipates on the first cross-functional team initiative. Another key signal is how participants' careers evolve after the initiative is
completed. More specifically, if management is serious about using
cross-functional teams, it must change the way performance on
these teams is measured and rewarded.

Empowerment. The most successful cross-functional teams believe
that they are empowered by management to solve their own problems. Empowered teams can work more efficiently because their
decision-making processes are greatly streamlined. However,
empowered teams can work only if management genuinely trusts
the team to manage itself. To be successful, the team must recognize the rare cases when it needs to involve senior management.

Deploying Project Plans

Although project planning methods tend to vary by company and
by industry, they share common objectives: technology leaders
want project plans to provide structure without constraining creativity; they use plans as a way of teaching new employees about the
corporate culture; and they want project planning to create a common sense of direction for project development teams. Microsoft,
Gillette, and Merck offer interesting examples of how to structure
projects.

Microsoft

Microsoft has a tradition of forging industry standards for desktop
computing that create sustained high returns for shareholders. An
essential component of its success is the way it plans its development projects. Microsoft uses activity-based planning that divides
its projects into three broad phases: vision development, coding,
and marketing. Its program managers develop a vision for the new
product by melding their knowledge of customer needs with a
deep understanding of the technology and where it is heading.

This vision is shared with developers. Developers are broken into
many small teams that write the code. These development teams
produce prototypes that are given to a select group of customers.

These alpha and beta testers offer feedback regarding product features and usability.

Each night the various components of the system are joined together through a "build" process. Bugs found during the testing process are then fixed by the subteams that are responsible for these bugs. This process is repeated until most of the bugs are eliminated or until management decides to ship the product, with the intention of distributing free "patches" at a later date. Finally, marketers introduce the new program at trade shows and develop and implement strategies to build revenues (from Microsoft annual report, 1994).

Gillette

The Gillette Company's Sensor shaving system was a successful new product introduction that illustrates the power of a focused product development process. In particular, this product's story demonstrates how a powerful external force can provide the impetus for members of various technical disciplines within a company to work together to create a successful new product. The Sensor was introduced in 1990 and by 1995 was generating over $2.6 billion in sales for Gillette. The initial prototype for the spring-mounted twin blade technology was developed in the early 1980s in a Gillette research lab in Britain. However, it took the threat of corporate takeover to galvanize the company into developing a new shaving system (Gillette 1993 annual report).

To develop the Sensor technology, Gillette scientists structured their research to gain insights into a variety of scientific fields. In particular, Gillette scientists studied the physiology of facial hair and skin, researched the metallurgy of blade strength and sharpness, analyzed the dynamics of a cartridge moving across skin, and gained insight into the physics of a razor blade severing hair. The development project also focused on how these phenomena could interact to create a better shave (Gillette 1993 annual report).

By coordinating with manufacturing, R&D engineers developed a custom laser welder for making twin-blade Sensor cartridges. The manufacturing-R&D team also created specialized scanning cameras for ensuring quality, which enabled Gillette to become the lowest-cost, highest-quality manufacturer in the industry (Ingrassia, 1992).

Merck

Merck organizes its product development projects into two broad phases: discovery and development. In the discovery phase, Merck allows scientists to use "rational drug design" techniques. Using these techniques, scientists experiment with the design of compounds that potentially can interrupt enzymes on the critical path of a major disease process, such as arthritis, heart disease, or cancer. During this discovery phase, Merck may allow several small teams to experiment with possible solutions simultaneously.

Merck has developed "combinatorial libraries" that allow for rapid, automated synthesis and biological evaluation of millions of compounds. This process helps scientists identify active families of compounds much more efficiently than a traditional "spray and pray" approach. Once scientists have identified an active compound, technical specialists work together to design a compound that does the job safely. After these specialists have developed formulations, process chemists design an efficient and environmentally safe manufacturing process (from Merck annual report, 1994).

By analyzing the common elements of Microsoft's, Gillette's, and Merck's project planning methods, several common principles emerge that could help a company attempting to develop an approach to project planning.

Common language. Executives create project planning methods to infuse a common language for discussing project work throughout the company. As a common language, the project planning methodology also promotes cultural values. For example, Microsoft's activity-based planning method reinforces the value Microsoft places on looking at projects from the customer's perspective. Project plans therefore have the benefit of teaching new employees how work should be done in the organization.

Risk management. Technology leaders define the phases of their projects to mark points at which financial risk is anticipated to increase. For example, at Merck, project phases are marked by decision points regarding substantial incremental capital and other resource allocations, such as for clinical testing, manufacturing, and marketing activities. The phases enable management to assess whether this incremental expense is warranted given the state of such specific trigger variables as technical feasibility, manufacturing cost, or anticipated revenues.

Project plans are less formal during the early discovery phases. At the beginning of a project, experimentation can lead to results that, although valuable for the company, may not conform to original expectations. As projects develop a more definite target, they require greater levels of capital and human resources in order to push them closer to commercialization. At this stage, the project plans gain more formal structure.

Methodology as a tool, not an end in itself. Technology leaders use methodologies as a tool for managing work, not as a method of control. Specifically, they adapt their project planning methodologies to the requirements of each project, cutting out steps that don't make sense. In peer companies, project planning methodologies may be followed with slavish adherence to policy, regardless of the specific requirements of a project.

Involving Early Adopters

Technology leaders involve early adopters in the development of new products. Early adopters are groups of customers that tend to be among the first to use a new technology. These customers tend to be highly creative and willing to work with technology developers to influence the ultimate design of a new product. Early adopters often drive the purchase decisions of mass-market "pragmatists" who seek the advice of the early adopters regarding which vendor makes the best product in the category. Heartstream, Schlumberger, and Intuit provide examples of the economic benefits that emerge from involving early adopters in the product development process.

Heartstream

Heartstream is a Seattle-based manufacturer of lightweight, easy-to-use, relatively inexpensive external defibrillators that can be used to revive an individual in the minutes following cardiac arrest. According to CEO Alan Levy, Heartstream worked closely with early adopters in its target segment of people who have suffered cardiac arrest in public places such as stadiums, airports, casinos, cruise ships, and office buildings. Heartstream's research indicated that the survival rate after cardiac arrest is 90 percent if a victim is defibrillated after the first minute, declining by 7 to 10 percent after each incremental minute. Furthermore, Heartstream found that survival rates varied widely by city depending on how quickly the EMT arrived at the scene of the cardiac arrest (1 percent survival rate in New York City, 25 percent to 30 percent in Seattle, and as high as 50 percent in Rochester, Minnesota).

Working with early adopters, Heartstream recognized that it could increase survival rates significantly. Heartstream developed a defibrillator that offered improvements over competing products in most of the features that customers cared about. Specifically, Heartstream's ForeRunner weighs four pounds, requires minimal user training, demands no maintenance because it self-checks, requires its battery to be changed once a year, and costs between $4,000 and $5,000.

Each of these attributes represented a significant improvement over traditional defibrillators. For example, traditional devices require extensive training and retraining every ninety days and demand battery testing up to three times a day. Furthermore, traditional devices weigh fifteen to twenty pounds and cost up to $10,000.

Heartstream is targeting a multimillion-dollar segment that it believes its larger competitors were late to understand and even later to respond to (interview with Alan Levy, Heartstream CEO, May 15, 1996).

Schlumberger

According to Brian Clark of Schlumberger-Doll Research, Schlumberger developed its Logging While Drilling product to meet the specific needs of its early adopters. Schlumberger listened to its off-shore oil drilling customers, who conveyed a strong need for lowering the cost of oil exploration. Fifteen years of depressed oil prices had caused Schlumberger customers to slash their exploration budgets.

In its market survey, Schlumberger customers also expressed the need for accurate, timely, high-quality tests. A cross-functional team of marketing and technical staff recognized that oil is typically found in thin, pancake-like formations that may be ten feet high and miles wide. Schlumberger's offshore drilling clients typically drilled many vertical wells through these formations.

Schlumberger developed a much more efficient technology that enabled customers to drill only one well. This Logging While Drilling product performs the tests that customers need and corrects the direction of the drill as it penetrates horizontally through the oil in the formation. This product enabled British Petroleum, a Schlumberger client, to save $150 million that it had allocated to build an island off the southern coast of England. This island had been planned to enable BP to extract oil from a formation using the traditional vertical drilling technology (interview with Brian Clark, Schlumberger-Doll Research, May 22, 1996).

Intuit

Intuit is a successful software company that uses a consumer products business model. Intuit recognized that word of mouth is a more important driver of consumer software purchase decisions than are salespeople, product advertisements, or even magazine reviews. Intuit engineers often change software in direct response to user requests. They devote substantial energy to providing customer support and using customer feedback.

As Bill Strauss, vice president of operations, pointed out in a 1995 Intuit corporate background brochure, "We want our customers to be apostles for Intuit. Our goal is to make the customer feel so good about our products that they'll go out and tell six friends to buy them." Intuit's "Follow Me Home" program sends an Intuit employee home with a new Quicken user to watch the initial setup process and take note of any confusion. Intuit subjects its products in development to beta tests and intensive scrutiny by a full range of users, from novices to experts.

In October 1993, Intuit introduced its Usability Research Lab, a facility dedicated to enhancing the interaction between Intuit and its customers. At this center, focus groups and customer advisory panels provide input to the software development process from the prototype stage throughout the life of the product. Finally, Intuit's marketing and development teams scrutinize hundreds of customer comment cards and letters; the resulting information is applied to the creation of each new product (from Intuit 1995 corporate background brochure).

Involving early adopters in the product development process is a simple yet radical notion for many technology companies. The technique is radical because it suggests that not all good product ideas spring from the minds of scientists and engineers. The Heartstream, Schlumberger, and Intuit examples illustrate the many benefits of involving early adopters in the product design process.

Customer focus. Working with early adopters from the beginning of the product development process reinforces a powerful cultural change for many technology companies. In particular, it forces the entire company, including engineers who had traditionally been isolated from the marketplace, to focus on developing products that create superior customer value.

Speed. Working with early adopters from the beginning of the product development process shortens time to market through the reduction in mismatches between specific customer needs and the performance attributes of new products. For companies that follow the relay race approach, the product may interest the engineers who designed it but may require substantial rework to meet customer needs.

Switching costs. By working with early adopters in the development process, technology leaders build relationships with an influential customer group, making it more difficult for these customers to purchase from a competitor. A major component of the customer's cost of switching is the effort required to reeducate a vendor regarding the customer's detailed product requirements.

Linkage to mass market. By building strong relationships with early adopters, technology leaders create an influential group of potential purchase references. For many technology products, mass-market customers rely on early adopters to tell them which product to purchase. Technology leaders can thus increase the likelihood that their product will become the industry standard. If the company has engineered its delivery system appropriately, meeting mass-market demand can be highly profitable.

Technology leaders follow several operating principles for working with early adopters.

Keep an open mind. If the product development team does not believe in the value of customer input, the focus groups and customer interviews will not produce useful insights. Technology leaders truly believe that customer input is critical for the design of a product. At the same time, they take what customers say they need with a grain of salt. They get the most useful insights by observing how customers actually use a product or prototype.

Ask customers for specificity and ranking. Technology leaders recognize that it is not possible to incorporate into the product design such vague notions as "quality," "performance," and "service." Companies must work with early adopters to convert these ideas into specific, measurable attributes, such as "two failures per billion," "155 megabits per second throughput," or "answering the phone within two rings." Furthermore, because technology leaders recognize that customers are willing to make tradeoffs between these attributes, if necessary, it is essential that customers rank these attributes.

Create linkage between customer needs and product attributes. As will be discussed in Chapter Six, these specific customer requirements must be mapped to product attributes that can offer measurable value to customers. Furthermore, in order to create a product that delivers these attributes, technology leaders recognize that they must either possess, or have access to, the complete package of technologies and other capabilities needed to build such a product.

Using Prototypes

Technology leaders use prototypes of their designs beginning at a very early point in the product development process. In the sense used here, prototypes change form as the product development process advances. They may start as three-dimensional software representations of a design concept and ultimately evolve into a physical model of the final product. Technology leaders get specific feedback on prototypes from early adopters before too much money has been spent and revise the prototypes based on this feedback. They also solicit feedback from manufacturing experts to assess the feasibility of manufacturing the product in sufficient quantities to meet market demand.

Many of the examples described earlier in the chapter illustrate the use of prototypes throughout the development process. Intuit, for example, works closely with its customers to adapt its products to their needs. Microsoft creates a new prototype every night as it rebuilds the many components of the systems that it is developing. Hewlett-Packard, in developing its printers, built many prototypes of its product that enabled the manufacturing R&D experts to develop a product that was efficient to manufacture and that could be manufactured in high volumes with tight conformance to quality specifications.

Parametric Technology and Synopsys make software tools that streamline the prototyping process, resulting in dramatic reductions in design cycle times and product costs. Their ability to create value for customers has contributed substantially to their superior financial performance.

Parametric Technology

Parametric Technology, based in Waltham, Massachusetts, is a $500 million supplier of CAD-CAM-CAE software to automate the mechanical development of a product. This automation extends from the product's conceptual design through its release into manufacturing.

According to its 1995 annual report, Parametric Technology was the worldwide market leader. It was ranked America's best medium capitalization company by *Financial World* based on its five-year average return on equity, earnings per share, and sales growth. Furthermore, its stock price appreciated 4,667 percent between 1991 and 1995.

In addition to its highly aggressive sales force, a critical contributor to Parametric Technology's success is its product portfolio. The company's products help its customers reduce time to market, improve engineering processes, and optimize product quality (from Parametric Technology's 1995 annual report).

For Hughes Aircraft, for example, Parametric Technology's Pro/ENGINEER product helped Hughes's radar and communications systems segment to reduce cycle time by 40 percent through the use of a common database and three-dimensional models that enabled planners, mechanical designers, and manufacturing engineers to do concurrent engineering.

For Acer, Inc., a Taiwan-based leader in the global PC industry, Pro/ENGINEER reduced model design time by 20 percent, cut prototype development time by 25 percent, and lowered mold generation time by 15 percent. Acer can revise its models with a few mouse clicks, and Pro/ENGINEER automatically updates all associated engineering drawings, manufacturing assemblies, and other related documentation. By enabling all participants in the product development process to work in parallel, Pro/ENGINEER reduces cycle time and cuts costs, because parts are designed to be easy to manufacture (from Parametric Technology annual report, 1995).

Synopsys

Synopsys, based in Mountain View, California, is a $265 million leader in electronic design automation. According to Synopsys's CEO, Aart de Geus, at the heart of the company's success has been its ability to regenerate itself by investing in the next generation of electronic design automation software that leads to 10x improvements in productivity. Synopsys also continues to sell its current generation of products (Aart de Geus, personal communication, August 21, 1996).

As Synopsys's product literature indicates, in designing semiconductors, engineers develop "netlists" for semiconductor fabricators that specify how silicon should be etched to implement the chip design. With the register transfer level (RTL) software ordinarily used for this design process, 80 percent of the prototypes that are produced by the fabs do not work as intended when placed into the system in which they are designed to operate. The netlist and the prototype chips must then be redone. In contrast, Synopsys's behavioral synthesis software allows chip designers to simulate the operation of the chip within the system before finalizing its netlist, thus avoiding the high costs of rework.

For example, a designer of an ATM cell scheduler (a data communications control chip) used Synopsys's Behavioral Compiler to reduce the design time for a 17,000-gate semiconductor from six to two weeks. Another designer of an MPEG-2 color space converter, a chip used to store color images that are transmitted over the Internet, reduced the design time of a 10,000-gate chip from twelve to two weeks (from Synopsys product literature, 1996).

Clearly, prototypes can confer competitive advantages on companies that use them. There are other important benefits when technology leaders use prototypes, including the following.

Customer feedback. Technology leaders use prototypes to get customer feedback early in the design process. This feedback is often more powerful than verbal descriptions of desired product features because it reflects how customers will actually use an early version of the product. This concrete feedback often drives the redesign.

Team building. Sharing a common representation of the product that the team is developing helps the team feel that it is operating on a "level playing field." In peer companies, each function may have a different version of the engineering drawing, with engineering perhaps holding onto the most recent version, and other functions, such as manufacturing, using an earlier version. Different versions often reinforce interdepartmental distrust or, at the very least, cause delays as groups with earlier versions acquaint themselves with the most recent version.

Early problem identification. Prototypes help team members identify problems with a design before it has been finalized. Prototypes create a forum for identifying and resolving problems before substantial capital and other resources have been spent.

Concurrent engineering. Building prototypes permits many different teams to perform their work in parallel. A danger of concurrent engineering is that the subteams are not properly coordinated, leading to local optimization at the expense of systemic optimization. By requiring nightly prototypes, as Microsoft does, project team leaders can achieve the cycle time reductions inherent in parallel work without losing the ability of the pieces of the system to work together.

Product Supply

As Geoffrey Moore observes in *Inside the Tornado* (1995), technology companies can experience a growth sputter after they have met the demand of the early adopters. In order to cross the chasm to the mass market of more pragmatic technology buyers, technology companies must identify an underserved segment that has a compelling reason to buy. If a company can provide a complete solution to this segment's requirements, the segment may then serve as a powerful reference to the mass market of pragmatic buyers. If the product achieves mass-market popularity in this way, the technology company may find itself "inside the tornado," transforming itself into a product supply engine whose sole focus must be to meet the tremendous surge in product demand.

U.S. Robotics (recently acquired by 3Com) followed these steps successfully for its line of remote-access products. Based in Skokie, Illinois, U.S. Robotics was the world's leader in remote-access products. According to Buck (1996), the company increased its market share of the high-speed modem market from 10 percent in 1993 to 30 percent in 1995. During the same period, U.S. Robotics captured 60 percent of the PC card market. Its $900 million in 1995 sales represents an annual growth rate of 91 percent. Furthermore, it achieved this sales growth while maintaining the highest five-year average return on equity in its industry, 28 percent. Its stock price grew 1,148 percent between 1991 and 1995.

The company's success was a result of its design architecture and its manufacturing ability. U.S. Robotics product architecture, unlike that of its competitors, used standard microprocessors and digital signal processors. This architecture enabled U.S. Robotics to bring products to market more quickly, lower overall cost, and provide a more flexible platform for customizing and enhancing products. Because of these features, U.S. Robotics was widely perceived as the industry standard.

Its competitors (Hayes, Microcom, Boca Research, Zoom, and others), on the other hand, manufactured modems based on data-pump chipsets purchased primarily from AT&T or Rockwell. The data pump performs the primary modem functions of modulation, demodulation, and error correction. Because each of these competitors used the same data pumps, they were all selling essentially the same product, and they therefore competed on price.

U.S. Robotics, by contrast, designed its own data pumps in proprietary software executed on standard chips. Because the data pumps were executed in software, they were easier to upgrade. For example, users could perform upgrades by replacing E-Proms, a specific chip, or by downloading new software from the Internet. The company could thus begin producing faster, higher quality modems even before they were 100 percent complete, knowing the company could easily upgrade to a fully compliant product. Furthermore, the company was not dependent on AT&T and Rockwell's schedules—nor on their higher-priced chips.

Unlike its competitors, U.S. Robotics manufactured its own products, enabling it to purchase its own raw materials, capture learning curve effects, and eliminate middleman overhead. This manufacturing capability also enabled U.S. Robotics to meet the tremendous demand for its products before its competitors could get products into the market. For example, in fall 1994, the company's V.34 Sportster, Courier, and WorldPort modems were introduced to market ahead of the competition in volume quantities. Rockwell and AT&T did not begin to supply production quantities until months later. In 1995, when explosive growth in the Internet and on-line services took place, U.S. Robotics gained an even greater lead over its competitors, who remained unable to keep pace with chipset demand (Buck, 1996).

U.S. Robotics achieved a position as the industry standard because of its superior ability to meet the needs of the early adopters, who in turn recommended U.S. Robotics products to the mass market. This example also illustrates the crucial importance of creating a product supply capability to meet the tremendous growth in demand that can range between 50 percent and 100 percent per year during the "tornado" phase of the market's development (Buck, 1996).

CEO Change Agenda

A company's ability to capture the benefits of a winning product development process, as described in this chapter, depends on two factors. First, a company should compare its product development process with that used by technology leaders. Second, the company should assess the CEO's willingness to lead change. If there are significant opportunities for improvement and the CEO is willing to lead the change process, the following strategic initiatives will be useful.

Pick a prototype organization. HP decided to test the new product development process in its Vancouver division. This division needed to succeed with its printer product as a condition of its continued survival, which gave the development team a powerful incentive to change in a way that would create value for customers. At the same time, all project participants recognized that they had the support and attention of senior management. The result was a new process that involved close cooperation between engineering, manufacturing, and marketing that led to a substantial new business.

Analyze the competition. HP was able to make a fundamental change in its product development process after it had identified a competitor that it truly respected. By studying Canon, a world leader in laser printer technology, HP created a focus for its change effort. In general, a fundamental change should begin by looking at your company strategically: examining in an objective way how it is positioned in its industry relative to its customers, competitors, and technology.

Reward success. Considering that the organization will be watching closely to see how management treats the participants in the prototype organization, it is critical that participants be rewarded visibly and that the success of the team should be incorporated into the company's success "mythology."

Let the change grow organically. After witnessing the success of HP's Vancouver division, other operating units began to emulate its practices. As these practices are adopted by other operating units, however, it is important to change performance evaluation and incentive systems to reinforce the new process.

Chapter Six focuses on how technology leaders sequence their activities to ensure that their new products create value for customers and presents the model of the "value triangle."

Boundaryless Product Development II
Creating Customer Value

At the core of every successful technology company is the ability to develop products that create competitively superior value for customers. Conversely, many technology companies fail precisely because they spend too much time on the technology and not enough on creating a product that customers are eager to buy.

For some technology executives, this distinction is beneath their dignity. For example, according to the *New York Times* (Markoff, 1995), at the end of 1995 Bill Gates had brought together a powerhouse assemblage of pioneers in computer graphics research: Andrew Glassner (recruited from Xerox PARC), Alvy Ray Smith (founder of Pixar, of *Toy Story* fame), Jim Blinn (from the NASA Jet Propulsion Laboratory), and Jim Kajiya (from Cal Tech). But the practical payoff for Microsoft's investment in research led the director of competitor Digital Equipment's research laboratory to sniff dismissively that Microsoft Research was engaged merely in "product development," not true research—as if to suggest that an absence of practical applications was the most desirable outcome.

Venture capitalists, on the other hand, do not share this dismissive attitude toward product development. According to Kevin Compton, a partner of Kleiner Perkins Caufield & Byers (KPCB), a leading Silicon Valley venture firm, roughly 95 percent of the business plans that KPCB receives are rejected because they are perceived as technology driven rather than market driven. Compton's partner, John Doerr, estimated that KPCB reviews some two thousand business plans a year, of which two hundred get serious consideration and only twenty to twenty-five actually get money (Peltz, 1996).

The recent history of video-on-demand and interactive television services illustrates how much money and effort can be devoted to technology in search of a market. According to the *Wall Street Journal* (Cauley, 1996), in early 1994, many regional telecommunications and cable television companies announced strategic alliances to take advantage of the "coming boom" in video-on-demand services. Interactive TV trials were announced with great fanfare in regional markets throughout the United States.

Behind the hype was the Baby Bells' fear that cable companies would use video-on-demand to get a foothold in the local telephone market. Their willingness to pursue these alliances sprung, in part, from a desire to keep cable companies from taking their customers.

As of December 1996, none of these ventures had produced favorable returns. In that month, Bell Atlantic, Nynex, and Pacific Telesis Group took steps to pull the plug on Tele-TV. It was estimated that the companies had invested roughly half a billion dollars over two years in this interactive television venture. Why did they pull out? Technical difficulties, rising costs, and vast changes in the market all contributed to their decision.

When the deal was originally announced, the participants thought that the Information Highway would be fiber-optic TV systems. Two years later, it had become clear that the Information Highway was the Internet. It also turned out to be much more difficult and expensive than originally thought to build the fiber-optic TV system (the three companies had originally split a $300 million investment). In the interim, Congress passed telecommunications legislation that allowed the Baby Bells to enter the $70 billion long distance market. The three companies decided it would be better to close down the venture and try for a piece of the long distance market instead.

A 1995 Unisys study of business and residential customers (cited in "Survey: . . . ," 1995) suggested another problem with such interactive TV services: *customers didn't want them.* The Unisys survey indicated that the vast majority of residential customers simply want their basic phone service to work right. Customers asked for accurate bills, no breakdowns, one-call problem resolution, and fraud protection. By contrast, only 16 percent said that services such as video-on-demand were very important to them.

Efforts by these telecommunications companies to introduce videotex (a kiosk-based consumer information service) into the U.S. market met a similar fate. In short, technology-driven products and services often consume tremendous capital resources without yielding a return.

The Value Triangle

This chapter shows how technology leaders avoid this common trap: by connecting the corners of the "value triangle," illustrated in Figure 6.1. The first corner of the value triangle is the specific, ranked needs of target customers; the second corner is the attributes of the company's product; and the third corner is the firm's technologies and other capabilities.

The key to the value triangle is the sequence that firms use to connect the corners. Technology leaders connect the corners in a clockwise direction (as shown in Figure 6.1). First, they listen to their target customers to understand their needs. Next, they connect the first and second corners by choosing product attributes that meet these customer needs *better than competing products.* Fi-

Figure 6.1. The Value Triangle (Clockwise).

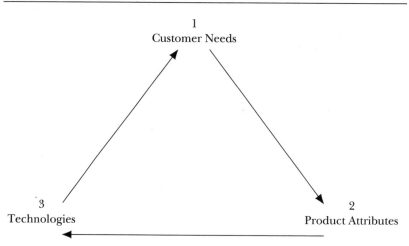

nally, they connect the second and third corners by developing, or bringing in, the technologies and other capabilities required to realize these superior product attributes. Because the product attributes outperform the competition in meeting customer needs, and the technology delivers these product attributes, it follows that the technology meets customer needs.

Peer companies, on the other hand, connect the corners in the counterclockwise direction, as illustrated in Figure 6.2. First, engineers and scientists tinker with technologies that they find interesting (the third corner). Next, they loosely connect the second and third corners by building a prototype that uses the technology that they think could make a good product. Finally, they loosely connect the first and second corners by seeking out a business unit willing to see if some customers have any interest in the prototype.

Usually this sequence doesn't work. In the unusual case where it does work, the technology just happens to meet a customer need in a competitively unique way. The dotted line in Figure 6.2 suggests that this connection is made very infrequently when the corners of the value triangle are connected counterclockwise.

If a company connects the corners in the clockwise direction, it wins. If it connects them in the counterclockwise direction, it usually loses. The case of Tele-TV is a variant on the counterclockwise

Figure 6.2. The Value Triangle (Counterclockwise).

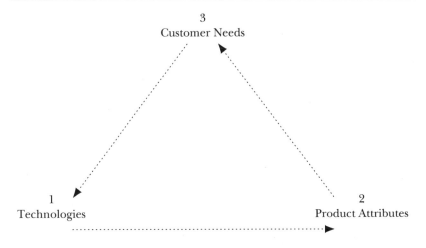

model. The Baby Bells were afraid of losing their customers to the cable companies. They looked at what the cable companies were trying to do, namely, upgrade their networks to handle telephone calls. And they invested in technology to support viewer ordering of movies on demand, which *they thought* would be better for customers.

The Baby Bells first studied the second corner, the product attributes of competing products. They then went to the third corner, investing in technology and other capabilities, without ever touching the first corner, understanding customer needs. The assumption that companies know what customers want is the biggest impediment to market success. Let's look at an example of what happens when a company connects the corners clockwise.

EMC Corporation is a $2 billion technology leader. Its return on equity between 1990 to 1995 averaged 41 percent, the top in its industry. During the same period, EMC's stock price increased 1,165 percent.

EMC took on IBM in the information storage and retrieval market and won. In 1990, IBM controlled 75 percent of the market, while EMC was not a player. By 1995, EMC had outmaneuvered IBM and others to take first place in this market (DePompa, 1995).

EMC started in the early 1980s as a vendor of memory boards for minicomputers. In 1988, EMC hired Mike Ruettgers as executive vice president of operations and customer service and promoted him to president and chief operating officer in 1989.

EMC's dramatic surge resulted from three crucial insights. First, EMC realized that mainframe storage customers wanted cheaper, faster, more reliable storage systems. Second, EMC understood that IBM, the market leader, was so caught up in its internal conflicts that it would be unable to meet these customer needs. In particular, EMC recognized that the low end of small-capacity-mainframe user companies was not being served by IBM. So EMC targeted this segment to achieve its initial success. Third, after introducing early products that met with some success, EMC developed a radical technology architecture that exceeded customer expectations.

There is abundant evidence that EMC gives its customers what they want. In 1993, 1995, and 1996, EMC was rated first in product quality, support, and value for money over all other hardware vendors, according to an annual independent survey by IBM Mainframe Users Information Exchange (IBEX) of 530 sites (from EMC press release, May 1996). EMC beat out Hewlett-Packard, AT&T/NCR, Hitachi Data Systems, Storage Technology, Amdahl, and others.

Consider how EMC helped one customer, IMS America, to compete more effectively. IMS America produces sales reports for pharmaceutical companies. In order to grow with its customers, IMS needed to help pharmaceutical companies compete more effectively. To do this, IMS tailored its sales reports to analyze pharmaceutical sales data by distribution channel, geography, and other market segments. According to EMC product literature, EMC's product helped IMS reduce the amount of time it takes to produce such sales reports by 25 to 50 percent, as compared to the system that it replaced. In addition, the EMC system reduced monthly downtime significantly.

EMC recognized that IBM would have a very hard time mounting a competitive response. EMC knew that IBM used several different system architectures. It therefore took longer for IBM to develop new products, because different IBM groups were fighting for resources. In 1995, for example, IBM announced that it had canceled its previously announced plans to enhance the competitiveness of its product. IBM had intended to add to the RAID (redundant arrays of inexpensive disk) capacity of its 3990 Model 6 Controller, to keep pace with EMC. According to IBM, the plans were canceled due to "budgetary limitations and performance issues." This change in plans put IBM customers in the position of needing to add another controller, an expensive alternative, instead of simply adding drives, in order to increase storage capacity (Steadman, 1995).

To exceed the requirements of its mainframe storage customers, EMC developed a single product architecture, MOSAIC:2000, that enables the company to introduce valuable products to its target market segments (mainframe, midrange, and open systems) ahead of its competitors. The design groups for EMC's largest product family share MOSAIC:2000 across products. Thus innovations in one design group can be quickly transferred to the others. In addition, as new markets develop, EMC has a common platform that it can use to develop innovative solutions for storage management. Finally,

EMC has found that it is very difficult for competitors to use hardware innovations to leapfrog the cumulative advantages of EMC's software (from EMC 1994 annual report).

EMC won by connecting the corners of the value triangle clockwise. First, it understood what customers wanted. Second, it figured out what product attributes it would need to beat IBM. And third, EMC built a technology architecture that enabled it to realize these superior product attributes. MOSAIC:2000 technology gave EMC the ability to provide customers faster, more reliable data retrieval at a lower cost. IBM, tied in knots by internal competition, was unable to compete in the marketplace. EMC went from nowhere to the number one slot in five years.

Let's dig into the process of connecting the corners clockwise by exploring each corner in turn.

Understanding Customer Needs

Understanding customer needs is an unnatural act for many technology companies. In a typical technology company, the engineers and scientists are the principle product developers. They are trained in scientific disciplines and are rewarded for advancing the scientific state of the art. They genuinely believe that customers simply don't have the technical insight to decide what should be in a product.

One of the most amazing accomplishments of technology leaders is that they have figured out how to get their engineers to listen to customers. Even more amazing, perhaps, is that by listening to customers, these engineers have designed products that meet their needs. In earlier chapters, we saw how technology leaders such as HP and Schlumberger actually transformed their organizations to get *and* respond to customer input. In this chapter, we will see how Microsoft achieved this as well.

Technology leaders are quite adept at converting general customer needs into measurable, specific customer requirements. For example, International Flavors and Fragrances (IFF), a $1.4 billion (1995 sales) developer and manufacturer of flavors and fragrances, does it superbly. IFF studies broad social and demographic trends and figures out how these trends affect its product line. IFF is particularly good at translating broad social trends into specific, measurable consumer needs. Furthermore, IFF is skilled at developing products with attributes that meet these consumer needs in a competitively unique way.

For example, according to the company's 1995 annual report, IFF realized that demand for its flavor products was driven by the emphasis that consumers place on health, convenience, and lifestyle. In response to these consumer trends, IFF's customers—food and beverage makers—reformulated their products for health purposes. In the process, new reduced-fat product introductions rose from about six hundred to over fourteen hundred annually. IFF learned from its research that customers wanted a healthy way of replacing the taste that had been eliminated with the removal of fat, sugar, calories, and salt. To meet this need, IFFs developed Living Flavors. This product imparts to health-conscious consumers the taste of ripe fruit, vegetables, and herbs.

In its fragrance business, IFF has developed a proprietary methodology, called "Mood Mapping," that links fragrances to the emotional effects that they produce. IFF has invested fifteen years of research in a system that measures emotional effects, from arousal to relaxation, that are induced by the company's mood-enhancement fragrances.

IFF measures reactions to prototypes by asking consumers to answer the question "How does this fragrance make you feel?" to specific prompts on a computer screen. Over the course of ten years, the answers to these questions have been accumulated in a database.

The IFF example illustrates several of the essential principles used to measure customer requirements:

Start with an analysis of broad market trends influencing the customer. IFF, Parametric Technology, Synopsys, EMC Corporation, and many other technology leaders gain insights into broad trends that influence their customers, and develop their product vision based on an understanding of these trends.

Identify the specific customer needs that these trends induce. IFF recognized that increased health consciousness had created a need to replace the flavors that had been removed from new products made without fat, sugar, calories, and salt. EMC Corporation helped its customers improve customer service and lower costs through quicker access to data and greater system reliability.

Measure specific customer reactions to prototypes. IFF's database of consumer responses to prototype fragrances provides IFF scientists with specific customer feedback. This feedback is used to modify fragrances to ensure that they match the targeted moods more precisely. An additional benefit of the database is that it helps IFF win competitive bids to supply fragrances to consumer products companies.

In the development of its word processor, Microsoft studied records of customer keystrokes. These records indicated that people frequently backspace to correct errors in their sentences. Microsoft also learned from talking to customers that they found the spelling checker to be too slow. In response to this customer feedback, Microsoft developed an auto-correction mechanism. This tool actually corrects the spelling of many words, such as "the," as they are being mis-typed.

Identify tradeoffs among customer requirements. During the process of developing a product, it is important to rank specific customer needs in order to identify potential tradeoffs. In many technology companies, design tradeoffs must be made between speed and price. A classic nontechnology example of a company's understanding of tradeoffs is Federal Express, who realized that certain customers were willing to pay a price premium for guaranteed faster delivery.

Choosing Product Attributes

In choosing product attributes, there are big differences between technology leaders and their peers. Technology leaders pick attributes that will make their products much more valuable to customers than competing products. For example, when EMC introduced its Symmetrix 4800 product in 1992, it offered a 67 percent increase in capacity over previous models at a 15 percent lower cost per megabyte (a measure of storage capacity).

Peer companies, on the other hand, pick product attributes that interest the engineers. For example, GO Corporation was founded by an engineer who wanted to create a hand-held computer operated with a pen instead of a keyboard. He raised $75 million in venture capital and employed hundreds of employees over the course of six years. Ultimately the company was sold to AT&T and closed down.

How did this happen? Enthusiastic venture capitalists enabled GO to survive without customers. GO spent years trying to sign a contract with State Farm to sell a pen-based, hand-held computer for insurance adjusters. It picked the wrong customer. And it was allowed to survive way too long without the right customers (Kaplan, 1994).

In Chapter Five, we looked at the powerful advantages of Heartstream's external defibrillator, the ForeRunner. How did Heartstream decide which product attributes to focus on? What technologies enabled Heartstream to realize these attributes?

According to Heartstream's prospectus, in developing Fore-Runner, Heartstream used its customer research to focus on five product attributes: size and weight, durability, maintenance requirements, intuitive use, and cost. In particular, Heartstream engineers were shooting for the following specific product attributes:

Small and lightweight. The ForeRunner weighs four pounds, less than half the ten pounds of traditional external defibrillators, and is the size of a hardcover cook.

Durable and easy to maintain. The ForeRunner was constructed with an impact-resistant plastic shell and a rubberized outer coating. It uses solid-state components and internal supports to resist crushing. Furthermore, its disposable batteries last for a year and are easy to maintain. Traditional external defibrillators require frequent battery maintenance. In addition, a five-state survey found that only 8 percent of respondents follow the maintenance procedures on traditional products (cited in Heartstream prospectus, 1996).

Intuitive to use. ForeRunner's icons, voice prompts, and text prompts guide the operator. Its proprietary PC training card facilitates convenient, one-time operator training. By contrast, traditional products use expensive and bulky training equipment and require between eight hundred and two thousand hours of training to interpret a patient's electrocardiogram (ECG) to determine whether defibrillation is required.

Relatively inexpensive. The ForeRunner is priced at $4,000 to $5,000 per unit. Traditional external defibrillators cost $5,000 to $10,000.

Heartstream was able to deliver these product attributes by developing seven key technologies. To illustrate how technology leaders link technologies to product attributes, we will examine the first key technology, Biphasic Defibrillation Waveform.

Biphasic Defibrillation Waveform is a Heartstream proprietary method of delivering waveforms to a patient. These waveforms are the jolts of electrical energy that are applied through the patient's chest to return the heart to its normal rhythm. A traditional external defibrillator uses a so-called monophasic waveform. The monophasic waveform generates current that flows through the body in one direction from one electrode pad to the other. This traditional approach typically uses as much as 200 Joules of electrical energy.

With the ForeRunner's biphasic waveform, the direction of the current is reversed partway through the pulse, enabling the ForeRunner to operate as efficiently as a traditional defibrillator with much lower energy (130 Joules). This technology contributes significantly to ForeRunner's small size, light weight, high reliability, and lower price (Heartstream prospectus, 1996).

The ForeRunner example illustrates how one technology leader connected the second and third corners of the value triangle. In particular, it highlights technology leaders' principles for mapping technologies with product attributes:

Link product attributes to compelling, unmet customer needs. Heartstream and EMC had a very clear understanding of how their product attributes helped to meet a compelling but unmet customer need.

Make the product do things that existing competitors will have trouble replicating. The Heartstream and EMC examples also illustrate the importance of offering dramatic performance improvements over existing products. Because of their insights into the strategies of their competitors, both companies knew that in order to replicate these performance improvements, their competitors would need to change their basic way of doing business. Competitor inertia can provide a surprisingly long lead time in which to capitalize on technology leaders' innovation.

Develop technologies to realize these ambitious performance parameters. Heartstream and EMC developed technologies that allowed them to implement dramatic performance improvements in key product attributes. As we saw in Chapter Three, technology leaders protect these core technologies primarily by investing to enhance their relative value to customers.

Use nonproprietary technologies where appropriate. To lower Forc-Runner's manufacturing cost, Heartstream used nonproprietary technologies for data storage and switching. U.S. Robotics also identified similar system elements, namely its microprocessor and digital signal processors, for which the use of nonproprietary technology contributed to the company's competitive advantage. The key is that technology leaders understand how each technology contributes to a product's competitive advantage.

Managing Technologies and Other Capabilities

Technology leaders manage technologies and other capabilities to realize the product attributes that create competitively superior value for customers. In its broadest sense, "technologies" refers to processes that transform inputs into desired outputs. As a practical matter, however, technologies often refer to specific scientific or engineering skills, such as C++ or Java programming talent. As the U.S. Robotics example illustrates, a key part of creating customer value is how technologies are coupled with other capabilities such as manufacturing, distribution, and sales.

Technology leaders have demonstrated the ability to change the way they manage technologies in response to feedback. In short, technology leaders are able to learn. In many cases, technology leaders have changed the way they organize and develop products to shorten cycle times and improve quality. Because your company may need to change in order to take advantage of the ideas presented in this book, it is worth understanding how technology leaders did it.

For example, it took Microsoft over a decade to develop the internal capabilities to deliver "zero defect" software products on or near the announced shipment date. Microsoft endured a series of painful failures before it made the changes necessary to produce high-quality software. The fundamental insight was that each day's code must be "built," tested, and debugged as thoroughly as possible before coding can continue.

In *Microsoft Secrets,* Cusumano and Selby (1995) describe how in 1981, IBM insisted that Microsoft improve its software development and quality control processes. IBM's demand came after Microsoft's version of BASIC, shipped for the IBM PC, gave the wrong answers when the user divided by .1. In that year, Microsoft hired Arthur Andersen to test its new version of the Multiplan spreadsheet for Apple's Macintosh before it shipped in January 1984. A serious, data-destroying bug forced the company to ship an update to Multiplan's twenty thousand buyers at a cost of $10 each.

Beginning in 1984, Microsoft decided to separate its development and testing organizations. As the testing organization expanded, developers stopped testing their code. Instead, they "threw it over the wall" to the testing organization. In February 1987, Microsoft shipped Word 3.0 for the Macintosh, delivered nine months later than promised. The program had approximately seven hundred bugs, forcing Microsoft to ship free upgrades to customers within two months, costing more than $1 million.

Other Microsoft projects, except for Excel, were also experiencing difficulties. These troubled projects included a database program, a project management application, and a word processing project called Opus. In the Opus project, testers were finding bugs more quickly than developers could fix them. This problem made it impossible for Microsoft to develop reliable schedules or to set firm shipment dates.

Although Microsoft had little respect for IBM's bureaucracy, in July 1988 Bill Gates decided to hire Mike Maples from IBM's software group to obtain more management expertise. Technical, financial, and customer service problems continued. The third version of Windows in 1990 had bugs that included network troubles, mouse difficulties, and data destruction. Stock options, an essential compensation component at Microsoft, crashed in value as a result of delayed product introductions. Microsoft customers were confused and frustrated because of product delays and recalls.

Maples suggested organization and process changes to help solve these problems. He proposed creating smaller groups targeting leading competitors and products. The company created small groups that targeted such products as WordPerfect, Lotus 1-2-3, and Harvard Graphics. The new applications organization consisted of five product divisions: office, analysis (Excel), graphics (PowerPoint), data access, and entry (Works). These divisions became independent profit centers. They had self-contained resources for program management, development, testing, marketing, and user education.

Microsoft found that the benefits of creating business units far outweighed the costs. The benefits included continuity of resources, the ability to plan, a tighter focus on customers and competitors, and better management development. The costs of business units, however, included less efficient utilization of such resources as testers, and less sharing of code and best practices across business units. By 1995, the number of Microsoft software design engineers matched the number of software test engineers (1,850).

The new organization structure facilitated a change in the product development process. In the new process, each subteam in the development stage of the project was required to submit its code to a "build" process at the same time every day. The code was then tested, and bugs were logged and fixed by developers as soon as they were identified. Microsoft products were thus more bug-free and could be delivered much more closely to predicted shipment dates.

This example highlights technology leaders' principles for managing technologies and other capabilities:

Adding capabilities often requires systemic change. The Microsoft example shows how bad things have to get before some capabilities can be added. To Gates's credit, he realized that he was so over his head that he went to his nemesis, IBM, for management skill. Even then, Maples had to wait for things to get even worse before Microsoft was ready to change its organization and product development process.

Systemic change takes a long time. At Microsoft, more than ten years elapsed between the initial recognition of the problem and the company's ability to produce zero-defect software delivered when expected. Even within an organization as successful as Microsoft, costly problems had to occur repeatedly before senior management acted on the need to change the company's approach.

Positive change is often stimulated by external irritants. Technology leaders probably take less time to wake up and smell the coffee than their peers. External irritants may take many forms. For HP's laser printers, there was a mismatch between what the firm did well and the capabilities required to compete effectively in the consumer mass market.

For Microsoft in the case of Internet browsers, it was the success of Netscape, an aggressive competitor offering a better solution for customers. For Microsoft in the case of product quality and delivery time, the external irritant was repeated customer complaints and a drop in the value of stock options. Often, the way a firm responds to these external irritants determines how well it manages its technologies and other capabilities.

Connecting the Corners of the Value Triangle: An Example from 3Com

To reinforce the concepts presented here, let's look at how 3Com connected the corners of the value triangle by (1) talking to customers to understand their needs, (2) translating customer needs into product attributes, (3) analyzing the performance of competing products on these attributes, and (4) leveraging technology to create competitively unique product performance.

3Com is a $1.5 billion designer and manufacturer of equipment used to connect PCs into local- and wide-area networks. The process that 3Com followed to develop its network access server illustrates these analytical steps.

Understand Customer Needs

By interviewing its corporate customers, 3Com learned that the number of telecommuters and mobile workers had increased substantially and that high-performance network connections enabled these remote employees to perform productively (from 3Com product literature). 3Com also learned that different kinds of remote workers have different needs: business travelers need interactive access to e-mail, spreadsheets, presentations, and document retrieval systems; sales and service providers, on the road or at branch locations, need access to e-mail, marketing and technical databases, and specialized applications supporting their work; and work-at-home telecommuters and after-hour employees need access to the same computer data and applications that they use when they are in the office—virtually all LAN (local area network) resources.

Translate Customer Needs into Product Attributes

Customer needs must be translated into specific product attributes. 3Com identified four general product attributes that, if satisfied in a competitively unique way, would give 3Com a competitive advantage: (1) seamless connections for remote access to information resources; (2) security to safeguard critical data; (3) scalability (the ability to add capacity without replacing the entire system) for cost-effective network growth, and (4) fast installation and centralized management.

Analyze Performance of Competing Products

An independent network product testing laboratory tested 3Com's performance against two leading competitors. This test found that 3Com was the best performer in terms of the two performance attributes that were most important to customers: information download speed, and value.

Information download speed. This test calculated how long it took the three products to download a fifteen-page report containing text and graphics. 3Com's product was between 10 percent and 25 percent faster than the competing products.

Value. A value metric was developed that took price and download speed into consideration. 3Com's value metric was 50 percent to 60 percent higher than its competitors.

Leverage Technology to Create Competitively Unique Product Performance

3Com's superior performance in the independent product test was based on its selection of the right technologies. The faster speed and better value of 3Com's AccessBuilder are attributable to 3Com's choice of microprocessor, the i960 RISC processor. The selection of a RISC-based processor avoided the many disadvantages of the PC x86 processors. For example, in a PC, the highest-priority processor interrupts are allocated to refreshing the image on the computer monitor and managing the use of computer memory, causing PC processors to take longer sending and receiving data.

The RISC architecture, on the other hand, is specifically designed to be more efficient at data communication. Another company that connects the corners of the triangle clockwise is Cisco Systems.

Cisco Systems, has done an outstanding job of creating customer value. According to Cisco's chairman, John Morgridge, the most important element of the company's success is its deep belief that its customers, not its engineers, are the best source of new product ideas (John Morgridge, personal communication, June 14, 1996).

Cisco Systems was started by two Stanford University employees who developed and sold internetworking equipment for their peers and other universities. Cisco always had a tremendous respect for the opinions of its customers, and unlike many other companies, Cisco does not believe that it knows better than its customers. Cisco has instituted several mechanisms for gaining customer input:

• It holds focus groups with its customers to listen to their internetworking concerns and to understand their unmet needs. In these groups, Cisco customers are invited to spend a day answering preestablished questions. Cisco representatives observe, listen, and facilitate discussion about customer needs.

• It dominates Internet trade shows and runs tutorials and discussion sessions with technical people in its client companies who are key purchase decision makers. Cisco's "networkers" program is a two-way learning experience for Cisco support people and engineers and customers' network managers and support people. These technical conferences typically last three days and are attended by four to five thousand people.

• Its help desk conducts regular surveys to monitor customer satisfaction with each Web site transaction.

• Until recently, Cisco gave all its customers direct e-mail access to its product engineers.

Cisco is not "technically religious." In other words, it will build products using any technology that customers want. Furthermore, Cisco monitors customer spending patterns and uses its highly valued stock to acquire companies with leadership in technologies that customers want. For example, a customer told Cisco that it wanted to buy Ethernet switches from a small company. Cisco subsequently bought the company, which is now a $500 million business.

Cisco listens to customers to understand their needs. It then gets the technology that its customers want. Judging by Cisco's performance, the approach seems to work.

Chapter Seven shows how technology leaders allocate the capital and insight they gain from their successful products and how they place their bets on new ones. The chapter follows a specific pharmaceutical company example through all the steps that technology leaders follow to hedge the risks in their research portfolio.

Disciplined Resource Allocation

Technology leaders excel at betting. They look at their capital and people as if they were gambling chips. They know more than their peers about the risks and returns in their portfolio. When their information tells them to cut their losses, they shift resources to projects with greater potential. Perhaps most important, they learn from what worked and what didn't.

Technology leaders know that research can create new markets in ways that are difficult to predict ahead of time. Earlier, we saw the role of serendipity in HP's discovery of inkjet technology. Consider the example of light-emitting polymers (LEPs). According to a story in the *Wall Street Journal* (Strassel, 1996), LEPs are pieces of plastic that emit a colored light when placed in a thin film and charged with current.

Market. These glowing plastics could take a big piece of the $25 billion market (expected to grow to $42 billion by the year 2000) for TV and computer screen displays. How? LEPs have big performance advantages over the most widely used technologies, light-emitting diodes (LEDs) and liquid-crystal displays (LCDs). LEP displays, once fine-tuned, could be lighter and cheaper than current displays. Furthermore, they could allow users to roll up displays and pop them in their back pockets. They could also solve viewing-angle problems that plague even the most advanced laptop computer makers.

Discovery. LEPs got their start by chance. Jeremy Burroughs, a scientist at Cambridge University's Cavendish Labs, turned off the lights to leave and noticed a faint glow from his lab table. Because a glow was abnormal, he decided to see where he'd gone wrong.

Plastics are made of long chainlike molecules called polymers. When arranged in a specific order, polymers are good conductors of electricity. Burroughs had been experimenting with using plastics as semiconductors. He discovered that when they were arranged in the right sequence these polymers not only conducted electricity but emitted colors as well. By dissolving these plastic bits into liquids, spreading them over surfaces, and adding electricity, scientists can produce a glow. In short order, Cavendish compiled a set of global patents for the LEP technology.

How does the story end? Cavendish's company, Cambridge Display Technology (CDT), is licensing its technology to display manufacturers, including Philips Electronics. CDT has attracted such investors as Esther Dyson, a high-tech guru; the founder of Acorn Computer; Apple's ex-CEO, John Sculley; and Cambridge University. Many technical problems remain, and there are an estimated forty to fifty companies worldwide trying to solve them (Strassel, 1996).

Recognizing that research can often evolve in unpredictable ways, technology leaders place their bets through *disciplined* resource allocation. This chapter presents the five key principles that guide technology leaders and describes the seven-step process they follow to implement these principles. The chapter illustrates this process with a pharmaceutical research project example based on an actual consulting project.

Principles of Betting on R&D

Betting on R&D can be a very high stakes gamble. Although the level of capital committed to the research portfolio varies significantly by industry, for an individual pharmaceutical project, for example, it can take between $200 and $400 million over a period of at least ten years to develop a new product. And there are many things that can go wrong.

Similarly, the degree of rigor with which technology leaders adhere to the seven-step methodology also varies by industry.

Technology leaders in industries such as pharmaceuticals and biotechnology, which spend the most money on R&D, tend to follow each step in the methodology. These industries apply the most analytical rigor at the point where they must decide whether or not to spend the most money—before clinical trials, for example. They may be less rigorous at the pure research stage because it requires a significantly lower capital investment.

Software companies, on the other hand, do not usually risk the same amount of capital, and to that extent are not likely to devote management time to building decision trees. In summary, companies considering the adoption of the seven-step methodology should satisfy themselves that the benefits of better insight for decision making exceed the costs of performing the rigorous analysis. Although it is essential to follow the five key principles described in this chapter, the means of implementing these principles may vary by industry and by company.

Technology leaders, regardless of industry, manage their resource allocation processes at a strategic level rather than at a product level. In so doing, they put authority for research portfolio management in the hands of the CEO. Across industries, the five key principles technology leaders follow in order to manage the most significant sources of risk in their research portfolio are as follows.

1. *Eliminate rigidity risk.* Technology leaders recognize that success can produce self-satisfaction and that self-satisfaction can inhibit learning. Technology leaders guard against the rigidity and defensiveness that make companies unable to respond to fundamental shifts in technology, competitor strategies, and customer needs. In managing their research portfolio, technology leaders use market feedback to adapt both products under development and the organization's business processes to these fundamental shifts.

2. *Manage market risk.* The market for which the project is being developed may not be large or profitable enough to offer an attractive return on the project's investment. During the life of a project, substitute products, new competitors, changes in customer needs or bargaining power, and other factors can emerge that undermine the attractiveness of a market that appeared profitable at the start of the project. Technology leaders explicitly analyze the attractiveness of the market into which they will sell the results of

their research. This analysis quantifies the size, growth rate, and profitability of target market segments and pinpoints the underlying trends that drive segment attractiveness.

3. *Understand competitive risk.* The project may yield a product that does not offer enough customer value, relative to competing products, to gain a significant share of target market segments. Market penetration could be limited if competitors are developing products with superior price or performance, faster time to market, or more effective manufacturing and distribution. Technology leaders assess how well their future products will meet specific customer needs relative to competing products. They use this assessment to change products while they are still being designed. They also use competitive position as a screening criterion to rank projects in the research portfolio.

4. *Bound project execution risk.* The project team may not be able to execute its plan, or worse, may not have a realistic plan at all. Even if a project has clear objectives and an excellent team with adequate resources, the team may not be able to develop a prototype that demonstrates the performance needed to meet customer needs, bring the product to market in time to gain a competitive advantage, or manufacture and distribute the product to meet cost, delivery-time, and volume requirements. Technology leaders structure their research projects with milestones that permit management to make go/no-go decisions based on the project's performance at predefined decision points.

5. *Limit financial risk.* If the overall portfolio of research projects is not managed properly, projects with the greatest potential can be starved for resources. This often happens in peer companies because funds are being diverted for pet projects with powerful executive or board sponsors. In more extreme cases, as occurs often in the biotechnology industry, projects run out of money before they reach the stage at which they can generate positive cash flow. Technology leaders structure their research projects so that they have convenient "exit ramps" that permit management to break a project into a series of ten to fifteen relatively small (say $2 to $10 million) bets instead of one big, $100 million, ten-year bet. By designing "failure" into the process, technology leaders limit losses and neutralize much of the emotion associated with terminating a project. In addition, if an appropriate price can be set,

technology leaders often choose to license out a partially developed technology that no longer fits with their strategy.

A Method for Managing the R&D Portfolio

According to Dr. George Heilmeier, president and CEO of Bellcore (from personal interview, July 1996), in contrast to many of their peers, technology leaders have changed their executive mindset from an "input" to an "output" orientation toward R&D. After World War II, executives believed that superior technology had made an essential contribution to the Allied victory. Many executives, particularly in industries such as electronics, telecommunications, pharmaceuticals, and chemicals, came to believe that technology could make a similar contribution to commercial success.

These executives built R&D laboratories that mimicked what they perceived as the best practices of government research teams: hire the best scientists and engineers, give them outstanding research facilities, and leave them alone to pursue their scientific interests in the hope that they will come up with a blockbuster product.

Although this input orientation still permeates many technology companies, technology leaders realized that this approach wasted a lot of money and did not necessarily result in projects that helped the company achieve its strategic objectives. To remedy these problems, technology leaders developed more of an output orientation to managing their research portfolio, with the following objectives:

- Adapt the organization to shifts in technology, competitor strategies, and customer needs.
- Create clear linkages between strategic objectives, competitive strategy, and research projects.
- Make research teams accountable for producing clearly defined results and for meeting aggressive deadlines.
- Encourage research teams to think like business people by requiring them to analyze markets, competitors, customers, and the risks and potential returns of their research projects.
- Shorten the time to make licensing and other technology syndication decisions.

- Cancel projects that don't measure up to these performance standards.

As mentioned earlier, the full-blown *disciplined* resource allocation process consists of seven steps:

1. *Capture portfolio learning.* Technology leaders manage their research portfolio as a means of capturing organizational learning. While managing individual research projects and allocating resources among them, technology leaders receive feedback from customers, competitors, and employees that they use to adapt their products and business processes.

2. *Construct portfolio grids.* Technology leaders link research projects to competitive strategy by analyzing each project based on its placement in a matrix, or portfolio grid, of dimensions critical to senior management, such as project risk and return.

3. *Develop phased project plans.* Technology leaders limit the risk in individual projects by developing project plans with exit ramps at each phase.

4. *Estimate cash flows.* Technology leaders quantify the incremental costs and benefits of moving to each decision node of the project time line.

5. *Build project decision trees.* Technology leaders use the expertise of their teams, informed by external information, to create decision trees for each project and to estimate the probability of success at each decision node.

6. *Calculate portfolio value.* Technology leaders estimate the value of their research portfolio. They account for the chances of project success and the timing of the cash flows. Their portfolio value calculation adds up the uncertain cash flows for each project.

7. *Manage the resource allocation process.* Technology leaders shift resources into the most promising projects through a disciplined resource allocation process. When a project reaches decision points that have been anticipated in the development of the project time line, managers determine whether to continue funding the project or to move its resources to more promising projects.

Capture Portfolio Learning

An important benefit of the strategic approach to research portfolio management is the learning that it funnels into the organization.

If consciously managed, learning can generate different lessons at different levels of the organization.

At the project level, the team can learn more about research projects under way in other firms, changes in competitor pricing strategies, and changes in overall industry growth and profitability. Any one of these factors can affect the expected value of the team's project. Furthermore, a postmortem analysis of individual research projects can reveal opportunities to improve project management that could benefit the entire company.

At the core technology level, individual team members can discover new product or process technologies and develop know-how that has the potential to help other projects or even to enable the firm to enter new markets.

At the research portfolio level, changes in corporate strategy, driven by changes in industry structure and the firm's competitive position, can lead management to cancel an existing project or to initiate new ones emerging from a corporate perspective on the research portfolio.

The following procedure captures and disseminates portfolio learning.

Monitor external changes. As described in Chapter Three, project leaders and senior management should monitor changes in the competitive environment.

Track internal changes. Similarly, project leaders and CEOs need to monitor both the status of their projects and the development of new technology or know-how within the project team and across the firm.

Update project decision trees. Based on the intelligence gathered during these two steps, project teams modify project decision trees (see Figure 7.2 later in chapter) to reflect changes in forecast product revenues, success probabilities, costs, and other factors that influence the project's expected value.

Build an internal best practices system. Senior management can take responsibility for creating an internal best practices system that could be made available to employees through an intranet that is indexed by such categories as technology/know-how, employee, competitor, and customer. One measure of project manager performance could be the amount of new technology or know-how the project team adds to the internal best practices system.

Microsoft has formalized organizational learning at the project team, customer, and core technology levels. As Cusumano and Selby (1995) point out, since the late 1980s, Microsoft project teams have written postmortem reports on over half their development projects. These documents, read by executives (including Bill Gates), are intentionally self-critical and range in length from ten to one hundred pages. Typically *postmortem* reports address what worked well, what did not work well, and what the group should do to improve in the next project.

Microsoft postmortems contain several important lessons that help Microsoft improve its product development process and hence its competitive position. For example, the postmortem from the Word 3 project led to an important change in the development process from a breadth-first to a depth-first approach. In 1989 Microsoft shipped Word 3, a project that was four years behind schedule and that contained so many bugs that Microsoft recalled the product and sent free replacements to seventy thousand users.

A key problem with Word 3 was the use of a breadth-first approach: developers took a first cut at writing the software instructions for all the features in the product without integrating them. Efforts to integrate the pieces near the end of the Word 3 project resulted in new bugs, creating an "infinite defects" state. Microsoft decided to change its approach to "depth-first," in which a specific feature is fully developed and thoroughly tested before going on to code the next feature.

Another important series of lessons was learned from the postmortem of Excel 4. These lessons were codified in a set of "zero-defect" rules that Microsoft enforced throughout its development organization (Cusumano and Selby, 1995).

Customer feedback is incorporated into Microsoft's product development at several different stages. Activity Based Planning, Wish Lines, and Calls Data are all used to incorporate customer needs and complaints with current products into the design of new products. Program managers and developers analyze user needs, develop specifications, and prototype products during development. Usability lab testing provides product development teams with important input before internal alpha testing. Beta site testing and product ease-of-support testing also provide important learning for the developers before the product is released. Finally, after the product is released, developers field customer service calls, participate in situation room teleconferences, and review customer satisfaction surveys and product usage studies. Furthermore, development teams use marketing studies and software versions that record user key strokes to make improvements to early product versions (Cusumano and Selby, 1995).

Microsoft encourages *cross-group sharing* through several mechanisms. It holds management retreats annually. These retreats are useful but limited because they are infrequent and high-level. Microsoft encourages middle managers and other people to share what they have learned through regular lunch meetings among managers in the same functions across different divisions. In addition, developers and testers hold weekly meetings. Finally, Microsoft shares cross-group insights by copying all functional managers on e-mail messages that address topics of general interest.

Microsoft provides an excellent example of a company that learns from its projects. It has formalized its learning process without creating rigid rules that slow down the company. Microsoft identifies mistakes honestly and develops effective solutions without punishing the messenger.

Construct Portfolio Grids

Technology leaders use portfolio grids to screen potential projects and to help the CEO link projects in the research portfolio to corporate strategy. Portfolio grids typically use pairs of dimensions that are meaningful for management decision making.

For example, some companies analyze projects based on industry profit potential and anticipated competitive position. This approach helps management focus on what the company must do to improve its position relative to its competitors. Other companies, such as Genetics Institute, screen projects by analyzing project risk and return, an approach that, for example, focuses a project team on reducing the risk in a project with lower expected returns. Synopsys maps out its research portfolio based on technology stage and breadth of product line, an approach that encourages the development of a complete product portfolio for its customers.

Technology leaders recognize that good ideas can come from many places both inside and outside the organization. Furthermore, because the number of proposed projects usually exceeds the resources available to fund them all, these proposed projects must be prioritized. Technology leaders use portfolio grids to prioritize projects based on management's objective of funding a collection of projects that balance risk and return.

As Eric von Hippel points out in his book, *The Sources of Innovation* (1988), in many industries new ideas come from leading-edge customers. As we saw in Chapter Five, technology leaders work with early adopters to develop profitable new products. Project ideas can also come from path-breaking work being done by startup companies and university researchers, as well as from analysis of the broad trends influencing customers' industries. In addition, many companies fund a limited amount of "pure discovery" research, akin to the "input" orientation discussed earlier, that can occasionally yield valuable breakthroughs. Teams can use ideas from all these sources to brainstorm and make exhaustive lists of potential projects.

Because portfolio grids link research projects to competitive strategy, they are very useful for communication among functional specialists and to senior management. If good data are used to position projects in the grid, the results of the analysis have significant impact on resource allocation decisions.

When the portfolio grid is used to integrate the results of the analyses of industry profit potential and anticipated competitive position, each research project is plotted on a matrix that maps the industry profit potential (low, medium, high) against the anticipated competitive position (weak, parity, leading). Projects that do not fall in the "high profit potential–leading competitive position" cell of the matrix are likely to be screened out, unless they involve the development of technologies that are essential to the commercialization of more attractive projects. Because technology leaders believe that internal competition can motivate faster and better product development, they will often allow two or more projects targeted at the same market segment to proceed simultaneously.

As mentioned earlier, many technology leaders screen research projects using other criteria, such as risk and return. The specific dimensions that are used can vary by company and industry, but they should reflect the most critical tradeoffs faced by senior management.

For example, Genetics Institute, a biotechnology company, seeks to balance its research projects between "home runs" and "singles and doubles." Home runs are projects with higher net present value (NPV) but lower probabilities of success. Singles and doubles are projects with lower NPVs but higher probabilities of success.

If a specific project does not fit within the portfolio, management may direct the project team to reexamine the project to determine whether it can be changed to increase its chances of success. This could be accomplished, for example, by changing the anticipated means of delivering a drug from the subcutaneous (underneath the skin) method, requiring potentially a more technically advanced formulation, to the intravenous method, one that is less risky to develop but possibly less differentiated (from an interview with Dennis Harp, director of investor relations at Genetics Institute, 1996).

Synopsys attempts to create a balanced portfolio of products. The company seeks a fairly even distribution of research projects by stage of technology and breadth of product line. To achieve this balance, Synopsys funds some research projects that make incremental improvements in existing products as well as research projects that are intended to create products that offer customers the "next generation" of 10x performance improvements as measured by shorter time to market and lower costs. The breadth dimension helps Synopsys analyze how a new product will complement its existing product line and make it easier for customers to purchase all their electronic design automation products from Synopsys (from an interview with Aart de Geus, president and CEO of Synopsys, August 1996).

Figure 7.1 illustrates a simplified portfolio grid from a pharmaceutical company, based on an actual consulting project. This nine-cell grid positions three research projects based on the profit potential of the industry and each product's anticipated competitive position.

Project A, a cholesterol-reducing drug, was the only product that passed through the screening of the portfolio grid. In my experience, there are very few projects that fall into the "high/ leading" cell of the matrix. The challenge therefore becomes distinguishing between Project Bs and Cs, a distinction that can best be made by understanding the determinants of industry profit

**Figure 7.1 Segment Profit Potential and
Competitive Position for Three Research Projects.**

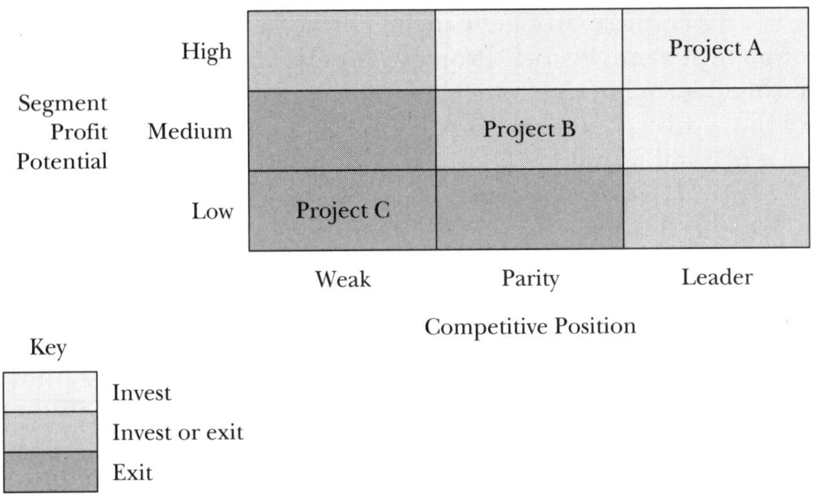

potential and competitive position. The details of the analysis include the following:

Project A: high profit potential, leading competitive position. Project A was a cholesterol-reducing compound. Its high profit potential resulted from the fact that it was targeted at a $4 billion market growing at 12 percent per year with an average contribution margin of 40 percent. The high contribution margin resulted from rapid industry growth caused by the aging of the Baby Boomers; market leadership from two strong competitors, the larger of which was working on a similar cholesterol-reducing compound; and the high distribution and manufacturing barriers to entry erected by these two competitors. Its leading competitive position resulted from its price, which was anticipated to be at 90 percent of the industry average; a 10 percent faster cure rate; and average ease of administration.

Project B: moderate profit potential, parity competitive position. Project B was an osteoporosis treatment. Its profit potential was moderate because it was targeted at a $6 billion market growing at 8 percent per year with an average contribution margin of 20 percent. The moderate contribution margin resulted from average industry growth caused by increased life expectancy of postmenopausal women, and from moderate distribution and manufacturing barriers to entry; these profit-enhancing forces were offset by the entry of generic competitors. Project B's parity competitive position resulted from its price, which was anticipated to be at 110 percent of the industry average; a 5 percent faster cure rate; and average ease of administration.

Project C: low profit potential, weak competitive position. Project C was a hepatitis B vaccine. Its profit potential was low because it was targeted at a $2.5 billion market growing at 4 percent per year with an average contribution margin of 8 percent. The low contribution margin resulted from slow industry growth caused by improved hygiene, the relatively large number of competitors in the industry, and the intense price competition. Its weak competitive position resulted from its price, which was anticipated to be at 120 percent of the industry average; a 10 percent lower immunization rate; slower cure rate; and below-average ease of administration.

As this example illustrates, analyzing research projects in terms of industry profit potential and anticipated competitive position is a particularly powerful way to link research projects to corporate strategy. This analysis requires the organization to address two key strategic issues: (1) Which market segments have the greatest profit potential for the average participant? and (2) What does the company need to do to ensure success in these segments?

Industry profit potential, a measure of the average return on investment of a specific industry or industry segment, is often used as a variable in screening projects. As Michael Porter points out in *Competitive Strategy* (1980), the profitability earned by the average participant in an industry is determined by the level of the five forces that influence the industry structure: rivalry among existing competitors, bargaining power of buyers, bargaining power of suppliers, threat of new entrants, and threat of substitute products and services. Management can affect the profitability of the firm based on the industry in which it chooses to compete and the choice of how to compete in the selected industry.

Technology leaders use the following process to analyze the industry profit potential of their research projects.

Segment the market. In firms that are technology leaders, project teams attempt to segment the broad market at which their research is targeted. Teams develop segments based on criteria that may include product categories, geography, customer industry, and level of sophistication.

Size the segments. Once the team has identified the market segments that it plans to target, it may be able to use data produced by independent analysts, industry associations, academics, trade journals, or even competitors' 10Ks to estimate the size of these segments.

Analyze segment growth and profitability. Using similar sources, teams can analyze growth rate forecasts for the market segments and estimate future profitability, as measured by operating margin and segment return on equity.

Understand the determinants of future segment attractiveness. Using many of the same sources, supplemented by conversations with customers, suppliers, and possibly competitors, teams can use the framework of the five forces mentioned earlier to pinpoint the factors that are most likely to influence the future profitability of target segments. These factors could include faster demand growth, decreased price competition, or diminished customer price sensitivity.

As we have already seen, *anticipated competitive position* is the second analytical dimension that technology leaders usually use to assess the strategic fit of specific research projects. *Competitive Advantage* (Porter, 1985) presents techniques that companies can use to improve their profitability rank within their industry. In general, Porter argues that companies can improve their relative position by configuring their activities in a way that provides customers with a superior "value proposition." In Chapter Six, we explored how technology leaders create products that offer competitively superior value to customers.

Develop Phased Project Plans

For projects that survive the portfolio grid filtering process, technology leaders create phased project plans. In Chapter Five, we saw how technology leaders use these plans.

Continuing with this chapter's pharmaceutical example, Project A's team developed a project plan that was organized around a sequence of steps, each of which required increasing commitments of resources as the project evolved into a marketable product.

Research. At this stage, estimated to last between three and four years, a relatively small number of scientists are assigned to perform experiments to design compounds that achieve price, contribution margin, therapeutic index, and ease of administration targets. In practice, executives rarely allow research to proceed for more than twelve to eighteen months without a go/no-go decision on a specific project. At the research phase, specific decision points can be established that help test for a compound's "efficacy"—for example, does it produce measurable treatment or cure of the targeted disease?

If after a predetermined period of time the team does not achieve results that are competitively significant, the project may be canceled at that point. If, on the other hand, the team develops a compound that demonstrates measurable performance improvements, the project is likely to pass to the next stage.

Clinical trials. Clinical trials are intended to identify whether the compound is safe. These trials are divided into sets of twelve- to eighteen-month periods, each marked by management reviews (decision points). In the case of Project A, the team estimated that clinical trials would take five years.

Because the risk and expense increase at each clinical phase, management needs to feel confident that the data emerging from the trials clearly support the safety of the compound. If the compound survives the various clinical trial phases, management begins to apply for regulatory approval for specific indications and to file patents on the compound and its "analogs." At the same time, if the compound passes clinical animal trials, management approves the expenditures for the next phase, manufacturing scale-up.

Manufacturing scale-up. As a company commences human trials, it incurs expenses associated with purchasing clinical materials, financing a pilot manufacturing plant, process development, and low-volume manufacturing. The Project A team planned for the manufacturing scale-up to occur in year ten. If the compound could be manufactured safely and efficiently, management was anticipated to approve the project into the prelaunch marketing phase.

Often a safe, efficacious compound cannot be manufactured efficiently, and the project must be canceled. For example, a company discovered a technique for removing an undesirable compound from a food product that cost roughly $1 per pound at the retail level. Unfortunately, the process for producing this desirable product cost between $8 and $12 per pound, resulting in the cancellation of the project.

Prelaunch marketing. Prior to launching the product, researchers publish articles in influential journals and the company makes clinical trial data available to doctors and managed care companies, distributes samples, and places advertising. Project A's team planned for this stage to occur in year ten.

Launch. The team planned for Project A to be launched in year eleven and to have a thirteen-year life.

Estimate Cash Flows

Having developed project time lines, technology leaders require their project teams to quantify the incremental net cash flows associated with moving through each project phase. (Until the project becomes a launched product, however, these net cash flows are, in fact, cash outflows.)

As with any forecast, the quality of the numbers depends on the assumptions on which the numbers are based. It is essential for all functions to understand and agree on the basic cash flow assumptions associated with their projects. Although this review process is often time-consuming and tedious, it leads to a consensus that is essential for achieving a sense of project ownership.

For example, the Project A team used activity-based costing to estimate the cost of research at $12 million over three years. This estimate comprised the following components:

Cardiovascular disease specialists: $4.4 million. This estimate assumed six cardiovascular disease researchers working for three years at a fully loaded cost per year (including direct and appropriate overhead costs) of $240,000 per specialist.

Medicinal chemists: $3.6 million. This estimate assumed six medicinal chemists working for three years at a fully loaded cost per year of $200,000 per chemist.

Enzyme researchers: $2.2 million. This estimate assumed three enzyme researchers working for three years at a fully loaded cost per year of $240,000 per researcher.

Additional research equipment: $1.8 million. This estimate assumes the purchase of two additional computers for molecular modeling and equipment for fluorescence ratio imaging.

Build Project Decision Trees

Having developed estimates of the cash flows associated with each project phase, technology leaders often build decision trees. Decision trees are difficult for team members to construct because they involve quantifying variables, such as event probabilities, for which team members have only an intuitive feel. By debating among themselves, team members can develop probability estimates and test them for internal consistency across projects. Through this process, team members gain a stronger sense of team cohesion and project ownership.

A simplified decision tree for Project A (Figure 7.2) illustrates how a decision tree might be used to value a project. The prelaunch cost of a typical pharmaceutical product exceeds $100 million. Such a product would have a typical life of twenty-three years, including ten years of prelaunch research and development and thirteen years as a product marketed in North America, Europe, and Asia. Because the risk of the project is reflected in the probabilities of success at the decision nodes, the cash flows are discounted at the risk-free rate, not the firm's risk-adjusted cost of capital.

Based on the assumptions and calculations described as follows, Project A has an expected present value of approximately $157 million. This figure represents the expected present value of the product's profit contribution after it is launched: $183 million minus the expected present value of the costs of research ($10.4 million); clinical trials ($11 million); and prelaunch marketing, sales, and manufacturing ($5 million).

Figure 7.2. Simplified Decision Tree for Project A.

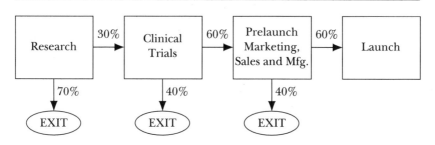

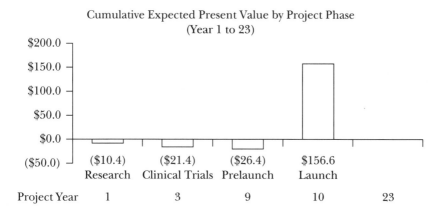

Research. As mentioned earlier, research was assumed to take three years and to cost $12 million. Assuming a 5 percent risk-free discount rate and that research funds are spent at the end of year three, the expected present value of research is –$10.4 million.

Clinical trials. The team felt that there was a 30 percent chance that the research phase would result in a compound that was considered worth putting through clinical trials (and therefore a 70 percent chance that the project would be canceled before clinical trials). If initiated, clinical trials were assumed to take six years and to cost $58 million. Assuming a 5 percent risk-free discount rate and that all clinical trial funds are spent at the end of year nine, the expected present value of clinical trials is –$11 million (–$37 million present value of clinical trials expense × 30 percent probability of submitting compound to clinical trials). Note that the $37 million is calculated by dividing the $58 million cost of clinical trials by the discount rate [1.552 = $(1.05)^9$], which reflects the assumption that these funds were spent at the end of year nine.

Prelaunch marketing, sales, and manufacturing. The team assumed that the project would have a 60 percent chance of passing clinical trials (and therefore a 40 percent chance that the project would be canceled before prelaunch marketing and sales and manufacturing). Prelaunch marketing, sales, and manufacturing were assumed to take one year and to cost $46 million. Assuming a 5 percent risk-free discount rate and that all prelaunch funds are spent at the end of year ten, the expected present value of prelaunch expenses is –$5 million (–$28 million present value of prelaunch expenses × 60 percent probability of passing clinical trials × 30 percent probability of submitting compound to clinical trials).

Launch. It was assumed that the product would have a 60 percent chance of passing the prelaunch phase (and therefore a 40 percent chance that the project would be canceled before launch). After the product was launched, the team assumed it would have a thirteen-year life, would generate average annual sales of $1 billion, and would offer an average contribution margin of 40 percent. Assuming a 5 percent risk-free discount rate and that total product contribution is received in year twenty-three, the expected present value of product contribution is $183 million ($1,693 million present value of product contribution × 60 percent probability of launching product after manufacturing pilot and market testing × 60 percent probability of passing clinical trials × 30 percent probability of submitting compound to clinical trials).

As mentioned earlier, decision trees can be used to quantify the changes in project value resulting from changes in external factors, such as regulations, competitive strategies, and customer needs, as well as in internal factors, such as the project team's ability to pass through project trigger points. For example, after three years of clinical trials, significant changes had taken place that reduced Project A's expected value from $157 million to $125 million. The project decision tree was updated to reflect the following changes:

Regulatory approval. During the clinical trials, a change in the regulatory climate in France raised the tariffs so high for the distribution of cardiovascular medicines that the team decided to exclude French revenues from the product's revenue forecast. This change reduced anticipated product revenues by $80 million, cutting the project's expected value by $24 million.

Competitive research. During the clinical trials, the team learned that a university researcher with whom they had negotiated unsuccessfully had signed an agreement with a major pharmaceutical company to push forward a competing project. In order to ensure that Project A would receive FDA approval before this competing product, the team obtained additional funds of $10 million to accelerate clinical trials. This reduced the project expected value by $8 million.

Calculate Portfolio Value

After the teams develop the decision trees for each project, management can calculate the expected value of the research portfolio. If the communication among project team members and senior management has been clear and frequent, the assumptions on which this calculation is based should be well understood and should appear reasonable to the organization.

This calculation helps assess whether the portfolio is creating value for the company and enables management to rank projects based on the value that they are expected to create. Management can also use the information to measure the depth of the hole they are digging with their research investment and to estimate the number of years of positive net cash flow required to dig themselves out.

The expected value calculation is likely to make people uncomfortable; this discomfort stems from the realization that when the research portfolio is reduced to a collection of risk-adjusted cash flows, its value is not as great as people had thought. Furthermore, research management may be uncomfortable exposing a previously protected enclave to the harsh light of financial analysis. Typically the "acceptable" way of expressing this discomfort is to question the validity of the methodology and the specific assumptions on which the expected value calculation is based.

The importance of consensus building becomes apparent at this stage of the process. If all participants have agreed to the methodology and assumptions, it becomes more difficult to undermine the credibility of the entire process when the results of the analysis are not as positive as people may have hoped.

Continuing with our example, the company decided to fund six projects for all its divisions, including Project A, with a cumulative expected value of $680 million. Although sensitivity analysis would be conducted on the entire portfolio, to maintain simplicity we will discuss only the three most important drivers of Project A's expected value.

Year three revenues. An analysis of the cash flow assumptions for Project A indicates that a 10 percent drop in the anticipated revenues in year thirteen would result in a 14 percent decrease in the expected value of the project, totaling $22 million. Based on customer analysis, the team believed that the most important factor that could lead to this 10 percent drop would be a lower than anticipated cure rate. In response to this finding, a subteam was created to monitor more precisely the factors driving the relative cure rate of the product.

Clinical trials. The model indicates that a 10 percent increase in the cost of clinical trials would result in a 4 percent decrease in the expected value of the project, totaling $6 million. The team believed that the most important factor that could lead to this 10 percent increase would be a two-year delay in Phase III of clinical trials. A subteam was created to identify and attempt to resolve any factors that could cause such a delay.

Prelaunch costs. The model indicates that a 10 percent increase in manufacturing costs would result in a 3 percent decrease in the expected value of the project, totaling $5 million. The team believed that the most important factor that could lead to this 10 percent increase would be an eight-month delay in achieving a successful manufacturing pilot. A subteam was created to study and if necessary bolster the company's manufacturing capabilities for the product.

To calculate the expected value of your research portfolio, use the following procedure:

Develop scenarios. For each project, develop decision trees that reflect an optimistic, pessimistic, and most likely scenario. Teams should identify the 20 percent of the variables that drive 80 percent of the expected value and develop three scenarios for these critical few variables.

Discount cash flows. Teams should use the risk-free interest rate, based on the treasury bill rate for the specific time period in the future, to discount the cash flows at each decision node.

Calculate expected value. Teams calculate the expected value of their projects by multiplying the probability of success at each decision node by the discounted net cash flow associated with that decision. To the extent that the team has developed optimistic, pessimistic, and most likely scenarios, management can calculate the expected value of the project and the overall portfolio for each scenario.

Perform sensitivity analysis. The nature of the sensitivity analysis that teams perform depends on the results of the expected value calculation. If the expected value of the portfolio is positive, the team may seek to identify the percentage change in the critical few variables that would drive the expected value to zero. Such critical few variables might include market penetration rate, success probabilities, gross margins, and manufacturing capital investment.

If the expected value is negative, the team could examine various scenarios under which it would be positive. These scenarios might include canceling specific projects with the most negative expected values, adding new projects with greater expected value, or quantifying the percentage change in the value of critical input variables necessary to make the portfolio expected value positive.

Manage Resource Allocation

Technology leaders manage resource allocation in a way that balances the needs of the "business" and the "scientific" sides of the organization. Technology leaders hold quarterly meetings to make key resource allocation decisions based on facts. They also hold more frequent meetings to encourage creativity in solving technical problems that may impede the progress of project teams that are seeking to achieve enough success to gain funding for the next key resource allocation. By making a clear distinction between key decision meetings and problem-solving meetings, technology leaders can satisfy the objectives of both the business and scientific communities.

Ultimately, the resource allocation decisions of technology leaders reflect the process of "directed evolution" described by

Collins and Porras in *Built to Last* (1994). Directed evolution recognizes that the success of research is fraught with uncertainty and that too much control can limit the potential results, whereas insufficient control can diffuse scarce capital and human resources.

Directed evolution is intended to balance the urge to maximize the amount of variation in the "gene pool" of research projects against the need to make efficient use of scarce capital and human resources. Based on the best information available, management continues to fund projects that appear to have the greatest potential value and cancels projects whose potential seems to have diminished.

It is this willingness to allocate resources—based on facts pertaining to market attractiveness, competitive position, and the achievement of project milestones—that distinguishes technology leaders from their peers. Over time, technology companies that allocate resources based on internal politics unwittingly liquidate themselves.

Continuing with our example, the project team presented its executive summary to the company's research allocation committee consisting of the CEO, CFO, CTO, and division executives. Project A was completing its third year of discovery research, and the team recommended that the committee provide funding for clinical trials. After probing the basis of the estimate of a 15 percent relative cure rate, the committee decided to fund clinical trials, at an estimated six-year cost of $60 million, based on the following elements of the team's rationale:

Cure rate. Over the three years, researchers had discovered a compound that inhibited the production of a key enzyme in the body's production of cholesterol. Based on preliminary testing in the lab, the team believed that this compound had the potential to drop cholesterol levels significantly, at least 15 percent more rapidly than existing treatments.

Ease of administration. Based on the chemistry of the compound, the team believed that it could be administered as a pill taken twice daily. This delivery mechanism would substantially ease the administration of the product compared to competing treatments, which were administered by injection.

Lack of competitive research. A review of the research portfolios of leading pharmaceutical and biotechnology companies, based on industry association contacts, consultants, financial analysts, and trade publications, suggested that there was no research being funded that targeted the mechanism that the team was researching. The team did find that a university researcher had discovered a similar mechanism, and recommended that the company explore a licensing discussion with the university.

Conclusion

The seven-step methodology described in this chapter provides technology leaders with six powerful advantages over their peers.

1. *Adaptive organization.* By updating project decision trees, performing sensitivity analyses on projects and the portfolio, incorporating postmortems into projects, and creating formal and informal ways to spread "local" learning across the organization, companies that follow this process build in the ability to learn from "failure."

2. *Profitable markets.* By supplementing the expertise of the project team with external research and by monitoring changes in industry structure, companies that follow this process can shift resources to projects targeted at markets with the greatest profit potential.

3. *Competitive leadership.* By monitoring changes in technology, competitor strategies, and customer requirements, companies that follow this process can shift resources to projects that are most likely to create leadership positions in markets with the greatest profit potential.

4. *Maximized portfolio value.* By cumulating the discounted cash flows associated with individual projects in the research portfolio, companies that follow this process can measure the expected value of their research portfolio. If the value of the portfolio is found to be negative, this process pinpoints the biggest cash drains, suggesting opportunities for improvement.

5. *Balanced risk and return.* Using the portfolio grid in the resource allocation process helps managers evaluate the extent to which they are balancing risk and expected return. To the extent that individual projects are out of balance, management can charge project teams with making changes that will lower project risks or increase their returns (or both) to bring them back into balance.

6. *Financial strength.* By breaking projects into manageable pieces, this process ensures that management harnesses capital and people in the most effective way, allocating resources to projects with the greatest potential returns. Companies can thus maximize their return on innovation.

Chapters Two through Seven described the four sources of advantage that contribute to the success of technology leaders. Chapter Eight integrates these findings by providing readers with a framework for self-assessment and an agenda for change.

The Innovation Scorecard

How can we be more innovative? This is the key question in the minds of CEOs in technology companies around the world. This chapter presents a framework that companies can use to help answer this question. It is predicated on two key assumptions: first, that innovation produces measurable economic value, and second, that companies can identify and improve the way they manage the business processes that drive return on innovation. To be fully useful, the framework must ultimately achieve the following objectives:

• *Develop a widely accepted set of measurements for return on innovation.* Some companies use percentage of sales from new products to measure return on innovation. This measure has many conceptual flaws. For example, the definition of *new product* can vary by industry and product line, from "products introduced in the last five years" to "products introduced in the last one year." Furthermore, counting revenues does not factor in the cost of developing the new products or the cost of manufacturing and selling them. Finally, counting new product revenues does not account for the cost savings or additional revenues that process innovation may generate.

As discussed earlier in this book, a more robust measure of return on innovation is the net present value of the cash outflows required to develop, manufacture, distribute, sell, and support a new product, plus the cash inflows generated by the new product. This calculation of return on innovation could be presented as a net present value amount in dollars, or as an internal rate of return.

• *Create control systems inside technology companies that collect data required to calculate return on innovation.* Because this definition of return on innovation has not been widely used by technology companies, people must invest the time to collect the data. If the pieces can be pulled together from different systems within a company, this may be accomplished more quickly.

- *Develop specific measures of the four sources of advantage that drive return on innovation.* The four sources of advantage described in this book—entrepreneurial leadership, open technologies, boundaryless product development, and disciplined resource allocation—are critical drivers of return on innovation. By measuring how well these management practices are being performed, companies can create an incentive to improve.

- *Create a process for benchmarking industry-specific best practices.* Achieving this objective could help companies learn from the success of industry leaders. In order to make comparisons among firms within an industry and across industries, companies should sample a significant number of firms. By building a sufficiently large sample, companies develop a meaningful basis on which to evaluate their return on innovation. Furthermore, the opportunity to share best practices will grow exponentially as the number and quality of the companies included in the benchmark database expands.

This chapter presents five clusters of questions that you can use to assess how well your company is doing at innovation. The first of these categories is the output measure, return on innovation. The other four categories (people, technology, product development, and resource allocation) measure how well each of the inputs are being performed. In reviewing these measures, you should bear in mind two points. First, the list of questions is intentionally broad. Individual companies should delete specific measures that are not relevant to their particular organizations and, if appropriate, add questions that may provide additional insight. Second, although the Innovation Scorecard can be a useful diagnostic tool at a specific point in time, companies are most likely to benefit from the Scorecard if it is used as a management tool over an extended period of time.

Return on Innovation

Companies use a variety of ways to measure the concept of return on innovation. In general, the greater the degree of analytical precision in the calculation, the less widespread will be the use of the measure. The advantages and disadvantages of various measures are described below.

Percentage of current-year sales from new products. As mentioned earlier, many companies use this measure to assess how well they are doing at innovation. This measure has the advantage of being fairly easy for companies to calculate if they track revenues by product. On the other hand, if a company generates 30 percent of its current-year sales from products introduced in the last five years, how is the company to determine whether that performance is good relative to competitors? Furthermore, if a company takes a year to develop and market a technology that it had licensed from a university researcher, and if this technology led to a $100 million product, its value to the company would probably be much greater than if a product with the same revenue stream had taken ten years to develop internally and had been introduced to the market eighteen months later.

Return on equity. This measure has the obvious disadvantage of being a very crude gauge of the value of investments in innovation. Shareholder's equity is allocated for activities other than innovation. On the other hand, return on equity, particularly averaged over a five-year period, is a good measure of a company's overall performance relative to its industry, and comparable statistics are available for publicly traded companies. To the extent that the company has estimated its cost of capital, the relationship between return on equity and cost of capital could be a useful approximation of return on innovation.

Profits per employee. Like return on equity, this measure has the obvious disadvantage of being a very crude gauge of returns from innovation. Relative profits per employee may well be driven by other factors besides innovation. On the other hand, profits per employee is a good measure of a company's productivity relative to its industry, and comparable statistics are available for publicly traded companies.

Stock price increase. To a greater extent than return on equity, this measure has the obvious disadvantage of being driven by factors other than the returns from innovation. Changes in stock price over, say, a five-year period are probably driven by many factors, including changes in interest rates and quarterly earnings performance relative to expectations. On the other hand, the percentage change in stock price of technology leaders tended to exceed that of peer companies over the period of time analyzed for this book. Furthermore, comparative statistics are widely available.

Return on innovation. The concept of return on innovation should be measured by calculating the net present value of the cash flows associated with specific product and process innovations. Although this measure has the advantage of providing management with an accurate accounting of the value that investments in innovation generate for the company, it has several short-term disadvantages. In particular, because this definition is not widely accepted, companies will need to pull the data for the calculation from their project budgeting and product revenue forecasting systems. Furthermore, it is unlikely that comparable data will be available from competitors and other companies.

Despite these caveats about each measure, they all have some value for innovation scoring. New product sales as a percentage of current-year revenue data may be available from your company's revenue systems. Industry and competitive data may be available from industry analysts or associations. Return on equity, profits per employee, and shareholder return data are widely available from analysts, the financial press, and company financial statements. Calculating return on innovation is likely to be a very time-intensive process for most companies. The steps described in Chapter Seven should provide some guidance.

1. What percentage of your company's current-year sales were generated by new products?
   Less than 10 percent   11–20 percent   21–35 percent
      35–50 percent   50 percent or more

2. What percentage of your company's current-year sales were generated by new products compared to your company's average for the previous five years?
   Less than 80 percent   81–100 percent   101–120 percent
      121–150 percent   151 percent or more

3. Compared to your competitors, how does your company rank in percentage of current-year sales generated by new products?
   First   Second   Middle   Last

4. What has been the trend in your company's return on equity over the last five years?
   Declining   Constant   Improving

5. How does this trend compare with your industry?
   Worse   Equal   Better

6. What has been the trend in your company's profit per employee over the last five years?
   Declining   Constant   Improving

7. How does this trend compare with your industry?
   Worse   Equal   Better

8. What was the percentage change in your company's split-adjusted stock price over the most recent five years relative to your industry?
   Less than 80 percent   81–100 percent   101–120 percent
      121–150 percent   151 percent or greater

9. What was your company's return on innovation, as measured in NPV dollars, for its process and product innovations over the last five years?
   Less than –$100 mil.   –$99 mil. to $0 $1–$100 mil.
      $101 mil. to $500 mil.   Over $500 mil.

If your company does not lead its industry in these measures, it may be particularly useful to analyze how well your company does on the four drivers of return on innovation.

Leadership

To answer the questions detailed below, a team could survey employees and managers to collect data on the effectiveness of leadership, the quality of the culture, the caliber of human resources, the extent of employee empowerment, and the motivational impact of financial and other incentives.

1. To the extent that you ask employees and managers, how many express confidence in your company's leadership?
   None   Many   All

2. What percentage of the CEO's time is spent with the chief technology officer?
   Less than 10 percent   10–30 percent
      More than 30 percent

3. How many employees and managers feel a strong sense of pride regarding your company's market position?
   None   Many   All

4. How many employees and managers feel that their colleagues are the best people in the industry?
   None   Many   All

5. What percentage of employees and managers graduated in the top 10 percent of their college or university class?
   0 percent   1–25 percent   26–50 percent
      51–75 percent   76–100 percent

6. How many employees and managers enjoy working with individuals from different parts of the organization?
   None   Many   All

7. How many employees and managers feel a strong motivation to outperform the competition in pursuit of company objectives?
   None   Many   All

8. How many key employees and managers work long hours in order to meet corporate business objectives?
   None   Many   All

9. Does your company provide incentives to employees and managers to learn about new technical areas outside of their field of specialization?
   Yes   No

10. How many employees and managers feel that they have the inclination, authority, and responsibility to make strategic decisions in response to changes in technology, competitors, and customers?
    None   Many   All

11. How many employees and managers feel that the organization makes a significant effort to minimize the "internal bureaucracy" that distracts them from creating value for customers?

None   Many   All

12. How many employees and managers believe that the company provides them with tangible opportunities to achieve personal wealth and career objectives?

None   Many   All

13. How many employees and managers receive compensation that is linked to independently administered surveys of customer satisfaction?

None   Many   All

14. What percentage of employees and managers are covered by a stock option program?

0 percent   1–25 percent   26–50 percent
  51–75 percent   76–100 percent

If your company answers None or less than 25 percent to these questions, there may be an opportunity to improve your company's approach to leadership. In general, your answers may indicate that your company tends to follow a somewhat bureaucratic approach to managing people that makes it difficult to attract, retain, and motivate the best scientists and engineers.

Technology

To answer the questions detailed below, your company could create a cross-functional team, potentially with outside assistance. This team could interview employees who are primarily responsible for technology management. The team could collect data on such topics as identification and valuation of core and noncore technologies; technology alliance formation, negotiation, and management; and outsourcing and outplacing of noncore technologies. The team might also review industry analyst reports on the company and its technology to supplement its collection of internal data.

1. How many times in the last five years has your company formally identified and valued its core technologies?

   0   1   2   3   4   5 or more

2. Does your company have a leading market position in any leverage-point technologies?

   Yes   No

3. If yes, is the technology *perceived by customers and industry analysts* to be the industry leader?

   Yes   No

4. Is there an individual or organization within your company that is solely responsible for monitoring new technologies?

   Yes   No

5. If yes, how many "paradigm-shifting" technologies has this individual or organization identified and helped the company to exploit over the last five years?

   0   1   2   3   4   5 or more

6. How many significant technology partnerships or acquisitions has your company executed in the last five years?

   0   2   4   6   8   10 or more

7. How much of a reduction in product development cycle time would you attribute to these partnerships?

   0 percent   1–25 percent   26–50 percent
      51–75 percent   76 percent or more

8. What percentage of current-year revenue would you attribute to these deals?

   0 percent   1–25 percent   26–50 percent
      51–75 percent   76 percent or more

9. How many technology outplacement transactions has your company completed in the last five years?

   0   2   4   6   8   10 or more

10. Over that time period, how much capital as a percentage of your total R&D budget was attributable to these deals?

    0 percent   1–25 percent   26–50 percent
       51–75 percent   76 percent or more

11. How many technology outsourcing deals has your company executed in the last five years?

    0   2   4   6   8   10 or more

12. Over that time period, how much capital as a percentage of your total R&D budget was attributable to these deals?

    0 percent   1–25 percent   26–50 percent
        51–75 percent   76 percent or more

13. What percentage of current-year revenue would you attribute to these deals?

    0 percent   1–25 percent   26–50 percent
        51–75 percent   76 percent or more

14. How many of your company's noncore technology alliances over the last five years were initiated with clear, mutually agreed upon objectives?

    None   Many   All

15. How many of your company's noncore technology alliances over the last five years were managed by executives with clear accountability for achieving these objectives?

    None   Many   All

16. How many of your company's noncore technology alliances over the last five years exhibited strong cultural compatibility?

    None   Many   All

17. How many of your company's noncore technology alliances over the last five years actually achieved the objectives set forth at the beginning of the alliance?

    None   Many   All

If your company answers less than 25 percent, less than 2, or None to these questions, you may have an opportunity to improve your approach to technology management. In general, your answers may indicate that your company tends to follow the costly and time-consuming "not invented here" approach to technology management.

Product Development

Your company may need to make a significant investment in order to collect "valid" data to assess product development. Specifically, the company could create a team to map the process for the development of a "typical" new product. This process map would trace the product development process. With the help of financial personnel, the team could identify the time and cost by department associated with each process step. The team would also collect data covering a representative cross section of projects to address such issues as project team composition and incentives, project planning, work with early adopters, use of prototypes, and effectiveness of the company's product supply capability. It could be helpful to supplement the review of internal operations with a survey of customer perceptions of these processes.

1. How many of your company's new products over the last five years were developed by teams with members from engineering, manufacturing, marketing, and other functional areas?
   None   Many   All

2. In how many of these teams did the functional specialists work together from the initial research design to product launch?
   None   Many   All

3. In how many of these research projects did teams work together to develop phased project plans with specific action steps, deadlines, and managerial accountability?
   None   Many   All

4. How many of your project teams received significant financial and career rewards for producing commercially successful projects on time and within budget?
   None   Many   All

5. In how many of these projects did teams identify and meet with early adopters to understand their specific unmet needs at the beginning of the design?
   None   Many   All

6. In how many of the projects were prototypes developed based on the team's detailed understanding of the unmet needs of early adopters?
   None   Many   All

7. In how many of the projects did project teams redesign prototypes in response to early adopter feedback, particularly after
   the first version?
   None   Many   All

8. In how many of the projects did teams redesign prototypes in
   response to manufacturing and purchasing department feedback?
   None   Many   All

9. In how many of the projects did teams redesign prototypes in
   response to marketing, sales, and customer service department
   feedback?
   None   Many   All

10. In how many of the projects did teams do market research to
    assess whether their product outperformed competitors in the
    attributes that customers valued most?
    None   Many   All

11. In how many of the projects did this market research indicate
    that the product did outperform competitors in the attributes
    that customers valued most?
    None   Many   All

12. In how many of the projects did the company experience a
    steady increase in product demand after the demand of early
    adopters had been satisfied?
    None   Many   All

13. In how many of the products that experienced such demand
    growth were manufacturing, distribution, and sales able to
    meet the demand without significant quality and customer sat-
    isfaction problems?
    None   Many   All

If your company answers None to most of these questions, you
may have an opportunity to improve your approach to product
development. In general, your answers may indicate that your company still follows a costly and time-consuming relay race approach
to product development.

Resource Allocation

To collect objective data on your firm's resource allocation process, you can again use a team approach. Particularly helpful here would be to compare projects that succeeded with those that failed. This comparison could pinpoint the best opportunities for improvement. Remember to reflect the level of risk in your industry.

1. Do project teams conduct postmortems after projects are completed to identify improvement opportunities?
   Rarely or Never   Sometimes to Often   Usually to Always

2. How frequently does your company use management off-site meetings and informal lunches to share learning across operating divisions and project teams?
   Rarely or Never   Sometimes to Often   Usually to Always

3. How frequently does your company use portfolio grids for analyzing corporate strategy?
   Rarely or Never   Sometimes to Often   Usually to Always

4. How frequently does your company use portfolio grids to screen research projects?
   Rarely or Never   Sometimes to Often   Usually to Always

5. How frequently do proposed research projects "survive" the screening process?
   Rarely or Never   Sometimes to Often   Usually to Always

6. Does your company use phased project plans that are organized to provide exit ramps at significant resource allocation decision points?
   Rarely or Never   Sometimes to Often   Usually to Always

7. Do project teams use activity-based costing to estimate the incremental net cash flows associated with each decision node?
   Rarely or Never   Sometimes to Often   Usually to Always

8. Do project teams estimate the probability of continuing and the probability of exiting at each decision point?
   Rarely or Never   Sometimes to Often   Usually to Always

9. Do project teams calculate project expected values by multiplying the probabilities and discounted net cash flows associated with each project?
   Rarely or Never   Sometimes to Often   Usually to Always

10. Does senior management calculate portfolio expected value by cumulating the expected values of each project?
    Rarely or Never   Sometimes to Often   Usually to Always

11. Do project teams perform sensitivity analyses of project expected value by varying the 20 percent of the input variables that drive 80 percent of expected value?
    Rarely or Never   Sometimes to Often   Usually to Always

12. Does senior management schedule portfolio review meetings to coincide with critical project decision points?
    Rarely or Never   Sometimes to Often   Usually to Always

13. Does senior management meet with project teams to offer advice on specific technical, regulatory, manufacturing, or marketing problems?
    Rarely or Never   Sometimes to Often   Usually to Always

14. How frequently does senior management agree with the resource allocation recommended by project managers?
    Rarely or Never   Sometimes to Often   Usually to Always

15. How frequently does senior management "kill" projects based on their failure to pass predetermined trigger points?
    Rarely or Never   Sometimes to Often   Usually to Always

16. Do project teams update the probabilities and net cash flows of project decision trees as new information is uncovered?
    Rarely or Never   Sometimes to Often   Usually to Always

If your company answers Rarely or Never to these questions, you may have an opportunity to improve your approach to resource allocation. In general, your answers may indicate that your company tends to make resource allocation decisions based more on internal politics than on measurable risk and return considerations.

CEO Change Agenda

The Innovation Scorecard can help companies analyze the extent to which they are following best practices in the management practices that drive return on innovation. If the Scorecard helps pinpoint improvement opportunities, it is the responsibility of senior management to take advantage of these opportunities. Answering the questions presented in this chapter can suggest specific management practices for which the benefits of change are most likely to exceed the costs.

As this book has demonstrated, meaningful organizational change is difficult but often necessary if a firm is to survive over the long term. The process described below has been followed by many outstanding companies at critical points in their history, yielding outstanding results. The example of the Hewlett-Packard printer, which created an $8 billion-a-year business for the company, was detailed extensively in Chapter Three. Ford Motor followed a similar change process as it developed the best-selling Taurus in the 1980s.

If the results of a company's Innovation Scorecard indicate that its return on innovation lags the industry, its CEO could take the following steps:

1. *Pick a "trial" division.* As HP did with its Vancouver printer division, a company could select an operating unit where competitive imperatives make change particularly critical. This division could become the site in which to experiment with and develop a new approach to product development.

2. *Build a "change team."* The CEO could pick a team including this division's executive and key functional managers. The CEO could supplement the team with an outside resource to provide structure, tools, and an objective analytical perspective on the team's work.

3. *Develop a change plan.* To initiate the team-building process, the CEO could give the team a deadline by which to produce a plan for changing the selected process, linked with the creation of an important new product for the company.

4. *Map the current process.* One of the first steps in the plan would be to map the current process using a recent project as an example to study. The project mapping could be supplemented with detailed tracking of costs and time for each project step.

5. *Study the process of "admired" companies.* The team could then identify and arrange to meet with companies that were selected for study due to their outstanding track record. Benchmarking could be arranged to enable the team to identify specific practices that could benefit the company. This data could be supplemented with the perspectives of experienced industry analysts.

6. *Design a new process.* Based on an analysis of handoffs and redundancies in the current process and the good ideas identified through benchmarking, the team could design a new process. The division team could then follow the redesigned process to achieve the project objectives.

7. *Train the rest of the organization.* If the new process produces a favorable outcome, the trial division will need to make itself available to other divisions seeking to learn from its success. By providing a living laboratory within the company, the CEO creates the basis for evolutionary change that helps the company enhance its return on innovation.

Chapter Nine concludes this book with some thoughts about the future. Technology leaders are bound to have an impact on the general business landscape and to affect the lives of managers, workers, consumers, and financiers.

Thoughts About the Future

This book represents the search for a set of enduring principles. If these principles have any value, they may have some implications for the future. In Chapter Five, we explored how high-tech products go through an early adopter/mass market shift. I believe that the principles that drive the technology leaders will follow a similar adoption path throughout American industry, and as these principles are adopted, they will affect the lives of managers, workers, consumers, and financiers.

General Business Landscape

Industries can be categorized by the basic elements on which they depend for their success. Arrayed in evolutionary sequence, there are four such elements: natural resources, manufacturing, distribution, and smart people. Over the last two hundred years, the "magic wand" of wealth creation has been passed from the people who control the natural resources to the people who control the smart people.

Obviously, there continue to be huge American industries that depend on all four of these elements, in a variety of combinations. However, the industries that set the pace for the rest of the economy are the ones in which the most new wealth is being created. And the most new wealth is being created by the technology leaders.

Because technology leaders are pacesetters, the management principles they follow are likely to cascade throughout the rest of the economy. It is unlikely that these principles magically embed themselves in every American company. It is more likely that these principles will spread first from the technology leaders to some early adopter companies, then outward to the rest of American business.

It is impossible to predict which industries and which companies will be the early adopters or how these principles will spread beyond them. One possible scenario is that the principles spread backwards through the evolutionary sequence of basic elements. In other words, other high-tech companies might adopt the principles first. Then such distribution-based industries as financial services and retailing, big customers of the technology companies, would adopt the principles. From there, the principles might spread to manufacturing-based industries such as automobiles and chemicals. Finally, they might be adopted by the natural resources companies.

Having spread throughout the economy, how will these principles change the general business landscape? First, large organizations will *dismantle hierarchy and become more flexible.* They will push real decision-making authority to the people who deal with customers. Everybody in the organization will be evaluated and paid based on objective feedback from the marketplace. They will have a real stake in the success of their company. Organizations will adapt to change more rapidly than ever.

Second, large organizations will *move in and out of markets more quickly.* As companies get better at learning, they will recognize that opportunities for profit in specific markets don't last forever. Companies will become more like arbitrageurs. They will get better at sniffing out profit opportunities and assembling the pieces they need to exploit them. Once the profit has been earned, they will move on.

Third, in order to move more quickly, large and small organizations will need to *learn how to work together.* The large organizations will compete for the new ideas generated by the small companies. The small companies will need the large companies' capital, manufacturing, and distribution. At the point of connection, then, large and small companies will need to become more alike in order to work together effectively. The success rate for these business alliances will need to increase dramatically.

How will these changes to the general business landscape affect managers, workers, consumers, and financiers?

Managers

Technology leaders will have an impact on managers in three important ways. Their practices will change the way companies manage people, change managers' attitudes toward organizational learning, and transform an understanding of how technology creates customer value into an essential requirement for being a CEO.

People

One of the reasons that technology leaders succeed is that they attract the smartest people. This simple idea is extremely powerful. In the past, companies won by getting a lock on scarce resources: gold, oil, or gas. In many technology-based industries today, the physical component of the product is a few grains of sand. What separates the winners from the losers is the intellectual content of the product, and this intellectual content comes from people. It therefore follows that the most successful companies will be the ones that get the people who can put the best intellectual content into their products.

As technology leaders grow in wealth, the importance of brain power will increase and spread throughout the economy. Companies that attract and retain the smartest people will prosper. Companies that cling to what worked in the past will rapidly fade away. Managers will need to create work environments that win the competition for the smartest people.

Organizational Learning

Technology leaders will use learning to get further and further ahead. They will keep their smartest people plugged in to changes in customer needs, technologies, and competitor strategies. Nothing will be able to stop these companies from getting more and more competitive. As they extend their reach into the economy, their ability to learn will create so much wealth that other companies will try to imitate it, so if you want to be on the right side of the power curve, learn how to learn.

Technology Skills

Technology leaders are making it impossible for managers to be ignorant about technology. The wealth of technology leaders will fuel their continued penetration into all aspects of business. Managers will no longer be able to hide behind a chief information officer or chief technology officer. In the future, managers will be selected based on their ability to use technology to create customer value. If you are an aspiring manager, you need to get comfortable with technology to avoid falling behind.

Workers

These changes will bifurcate the workforce. There will be a very small number of workers who make a tremendous difference to society, and there will be the vast majority of workers who live comfortably but unremarkably.

The most successful companies will compete for the services of an elite group of smart, technically savvy, highly energetic workers. These smart people will enjoy interesting careers and become quite wealthy.

The rest of the workforce will make enough money to live comfortably. Many will enjoy a better lifestyle because they will use home computers linked to corporate networks as a means of balancing their work and personal lives. But most workers will pay a price for this: their careers will be more mundane and their opportunities for wealth relatively limited.

Worker training will become more important than it is now. Schools will need to give people the skills that companies need in their workers. Elite colleges and universities will need to develop courses that give workers the technical and organizational skills that businesses require of their elite core. Public schools will need to provide the rest of the workforce with a more solid grounding in reading, mathematics, and computers.

Consumers

Technology leaders will continue to create products that improve the lives of consumers. On the other hand, some technology companies will churn out many products that consumers don't want. Of course the market will take care of these companies over time.

Technology leaders have conditioned consumers to expect more bang for the buck. It is likely that this trend will continue as long as more processing power can be crammed onto semiconductors at a lower and lower unit cost. At some point, however, there may be a huge time lag between greater CPU price or performance and the ability to develop applications that customers are willing to pay for.

Intel is beginning to feel this gap: Can new uses be found for all the powerful CPUs Intel can churn out with semiconductor fabrication plants whose construction cost is rapidly growing from $2 billion to $10 billion? With these cost increases, the number of units that must be sold to make a profit on the incremental fab goes up exponentially. Companies like Intel must invest in developing large markets that can consume the processing power they produce. Otherwise, the entire industry, as it is currently configured, could collapse.

Consumers will probably continue to have a choice of new products that give them greater value. At some point, the consumer market for technology products, such as home computers, will reach saturation. When this occurs, consumers may experience diminishing returns when upgrading. Simply put, if a new product or a new version does not give the consumer enough additional value to justify spending the extra money, most consumers will stick with what they have. As long as technology leaders can continue to create enough additional value to get consumers to upgrade, this problem can be deferred and growth can continue.

Financiers

Technology leaders will have a big impact on financiers as well. First, technology leaders will compete directly with venture capitalists. Second, they will create tremendous wealth for shareholders, so portfolio managers will want to own their stocks. Third, they will create technology that transforms the process of raising and investing capital.

Venture Capital

Many technology leaders have created their own venture capital arms. Certainly these companies have access to capital as a result of their enormous market valuations. They have two other critical ingredients: understanding of technology and markets, and managerial talent. This means the returns that venture capitalists can earn are likely to diminish as more competitors chase a fairly limited pool of good deals.

Of course this reversion toward the mean could be prevented if venture capitalists find new ways to compete. One such model may be that found at Kleiner Perkins. KPCB has invested in companies that potentially "own" critical components of the Internet business model. In other words, as the Internet becomes a way to make money, Kleiner Perkins will own equity in the most valuable pieces.

What is unique in this model is that the firm encourages different companies that it owns to do business with each other. This kind of firm can potentially create more value than could have been generated by a passive investor who simply bought and held shares in the companies.

One thing is certain, venture capitalists will need to come up with new ideas for how to compete in order to continue earning above-average returns. Technology leaders changed their fundamental approach to accessing new technology by getting into the venture capital business. Their entry into the market will force incumbents to change their fundamental business processes as well.

Investment Opportunities

The twenty companies analyzed in this book generated shareholder wealth at over four and a half times the market rate during the first half of the 1990s. Put another way, if an investor had purchased stock in the twenty technology leaders in 1990, their investment would have grown at a compound annual rate of over 180 percent.

Although it is unlikely that an investment in the same portfolio of stocks will produce similar results in the future, investors can still learn something from what made these companies do so well. Part of the answer has to do with buying the stock before the rest of the market figures out how valuable it is.

Technology leaders share five characteristics that could be useful leading indicators for a diligent investor. First, the company should participate in a market that is growing very fast. Second, it should be led by a CEO who combines a deep understanding of technology with tremendous business savvy. Third, the company should have a product with an outstanding reputation among early adopters and industry experts. Fourth, it should have a reputation among top engineers and scientists as being a great place to work. Fifth, the company should be profitable and have a balance sheet with lots of cash and minimal debt. As the first four of these criteria require some digging to get the answers, they could provide an advantage to a diligent investor.

Investment Technology

Technology leaders will create technology that changes the nature of capital markets. Just as technology companies succeed by hiring the smartest engineers, so do investment firms succeed by hiring the smartest financiers. In fact, over the last decade, the investment houses have been able to hire many of the same math and science Ph.D. graduates that the high-tech companies wanted to hire.

The competition among securities valuation models is likely to affect investor returns and traders' incomes. Since the mid-1980s, financiers have developed models that identify difficult-to-detect patterns in the financial markets. These patterns create opportunities to execute trades that take advantage of tiny and very short-lived mispricing of securities. At the core of these sophisticated models are a very high powered computer, huge volumes of accurate and timely securities price information, and a small number of very smart mathematicians and scientists who analyze the data to identify these investment opportunities.

As the power of the technology increases, these models will have much shorter "half-lives" during which they generate high investor returns. Thus the competition will continue on the basis of who has the smartest people, who has the best data, and who has the most powerful tools for analyzing the data to identify the investment opportunities.

Of course, technology will also reduce transaction costs for the more mundane parts of the capital markets. For example, at some point the financial advantages of an all-electronic stock trading system will overwhelm the political power of the specialists who control today's hybrid system. Fundamental analysis and real-time securities price information will be available to all market participants at a nominal price. Securities custody and accounting functions will be performed with tremendous efficiency. These process improvements will drive down transaction costs and reduce information asymmetries, making the capital markets much more efficient.

———— ∞∞ ————

To summarize what we have discussed in this chapter: the business landscape will become more efficient as technology leaders continue to make the world a better place, finding new ways to create greater customer value at a lower cost. Managers will compete for the smartest workers and create work environments that stress learning and adaptation. Workers will have greater freedom and responsibility in directing their careers. Consumers will be able to choose from a broad range of products that deliver more bang for the buck. And financiers will develop new ways to raise capital efficiently and invest it at high rates of return.

References

Alster, N. "Making the Kids Stand on Their Own." *Forbes,* Oct. 9, 1995. pp. 49–56.

"AMD Gains Access to Intel Patents, MMX." *Microprocessor Report,* Jan. 22, 1996, *10*(1), 5.

"Amgen Announcement of NPS Alliance." [http://www.recap.com/]. May 1996.

"Amgen Announcement of Yamanouchi Agreement." [http://www.recap.com/]. May 1996.

"Annual Report on American Industry." *Forbes,* Jan. 1, 1996, pp. 76–235.

Buck, E. "U.S. Robotics: The Leader in Remote Access Technologies." *Donaldson, Lufkin & Jenrette,* Mar. 1, 1996.

Cauley, L. "Bell Atlantic, Nynex, PacTel to Close Tele-TV." *Wall Street Journal,* Dec. 6, 1996, pp. A3, A10.

Clark, D. "A Dud at Its Birth, Windows NT Is Back As Networking Force." *Wall Street Journal,* July 29, 1996, pp. A1, A4.

Collins, J., and Porras, J. *Built to Last: Successful Habits of Visionary Companies.* New York: HarperBusiness, 1994.

Crockett, B. "Death for the gold-spinning, high-tech genie? Grove poses the question." *MSNBC,* November 16, 1996. [http://www.msnbc.com]

Cusumano, M., and Selby, R. *Microsoft Secrets: How the World's Most Powerful Software Company Creates Technology, Shapes Markets, and Manages People.* New York: Free Press, 1995.

DePompa, B. "EMC Is the One to Beat." *Information Week,* May 1, 1995. [[http://www.techweb.com/se/directlink.cgi?IWK1995050.50071]

Dolan, K. "Help Wanted: Urgent!" *Forbes,* Oct. 7, 1996, p. 18.

Heskett, B. "Cisco Buys Granite Systems." *C|net,* Sept. 3, 1996. [http://www.news.com/News/Item/0,4,3000,00.html]

"HP Labs." [http://www.hp.com/abouthp/hplabs.htm]. Mar. 1995.

Ingrassia, L. "The Cutting Edge." *Wall Street Journal,* Apr. 6, 1992, p. R6.

Kaplan, J. *Startup: A Silicon Valley Adventure.* New York: Penguin Books, 1994.

Klaus, T. "Checking Out Linux." *UnixWorld,* Mar. 1993, p. 66.

Lenzner, R. "The Reluctant Entrepreneur." *Forbes,* Sept. 11, 1995, p. 162.

Levine, J. "'A' Is for Arbitrage." *Forbes,* July 15, 1996, pp. 116–121.

Loeb, M. "Ten Commandments for Managing Creative People." *Fortune,* Jan. 16, 1995, pp. 135–136.

Markoff, J. "Microsoft Quietly Puts Together Computer Research Laboratory." *New York Times,* Dec. 11, 1995, pp. D1, D5.

Michaels, J. "Keeping Score." *Forbes,* Oct. 14, 1996, p. 16.

"Microsoft Incorporates Java as a Feature of Windows." [Microsoft press release], April 30, 1996. [http://www.Microsoft.com/corpinfo/press/1996/apr1996/actxjapr.htm]

Mitchell, J. "Standards, Integrity, and Concern for Employees." *San Jose Mercury News,* March 27, 1996 [http://www.sjmercury.com/business/packard/standard.htm].

Moore, G. *Inside the Tornado.* New York: HarperBusiness, 1995.

Nee, E. "Interview with John Chambers." *Upside,* July 1996. [http://www.upside.com/texis/archive/search/article.html?U1D=9607011011]

"Patents: Bay Networks and 3Com Corporation Announce Patent Cross-Licensing Pact." *EDGE: Work-Group Computing Report,* Nov. 27, 1995, *6*(289), 15.

Peltz, M. "High Tech's Premier Venture Capitalist." *Institutional Investor,* June 1996, p. 92.

Porter, M. *Competitive Strategy: Techniques for Analyzing Industries and Competitors.* New York: Free Press, 1980.

Porter, M. *Competitive Advantage: Creating and Sustaining Superior Performance.* New York: Free Press, 1985.

"Quotes on David Packard." *San Jose Mercury News,* Mar. 27, 1996. [http://www.sjmercury.com/business/packard/quotes.htm]

Seabrook, J. "E-Mail from Bill." *New Yorker,* Jan. 10, 1994, p. 59.

Steadman, C. "IBM Drops RAID Boost; Costs, Complexity May Rise." *Computerworld,* Feb. 20, 1995. [http://www.computerworld.com/search/AT-html/9502/950220SL7ibmraid.html]

Stephens, M. "Revenge of the Nerds." [PBS television broadcast], October 1996.

Strassel, K. "Liquid Plastic May Transform TV Screens." *Wall Street Journal,* Dec. 3, 1996, p. 86.

Stross, R. *The Microsoft Way: The Real Story of How the Company Outsmarts Its Competition.* Reading, Mass.: Addison-Wesley, 1996.

"Survey: Unisys/Telephony Magazine Survey on Customer Service and Buyer Values Points to Winners of the Telephone Wars: Long Distance, Local Telephone, Cable TV and Cellular Companies Getting into Each Other's Business." *EDGE: On and About AT&T,* Nov. 13, 1995, *10*(138), 8.

Tanouye, E. "Value of Some Drug Firms' Acquisitions Is Questioned." *Wall Street Journal,* Nov. 19, 1996, p. B4.

Trachtenberg, J. "How Philips Flubbed Its U.S. Introduction of Electronic Product." *Wall Street Journal,* June 28, 1996, pp. A1, A4.

Yoder, S. "How H-P Used Tactics of the Japanese to Beat Them at Their Game." *Wall Street Journal,* Sept. 8, 1994, pp. A1, A9.

von Hippel, E. *The Sources of Innovation.* New York: Oxford University Press, 1988.

Wilke, J. "Thermo Electron Uses an Unusual Strategy to Create Products." *Wall Street Journal,* Aug. 5, 1993, pp. A1, A7.

Index